ABCDE

GHIJKM

Alphamaniacs

BUILDERS OF 26 WONDERS

OF THE

WORD

In memory of four fine alphamaniacs:

Arthur Bronstein, Gary Cooke, Bob Goldfarb, and Annette LeSiege

For Jack, writer and wordsmith

Baird, Jessie Little Doe. Excerpt from Wôpanâak Language Reclamation Project. www.wlrp.org.
Used by permission of Jessie Little Doe Baird.

Bauby, Jean-Dominque. Excerpts from *The Diving Bell and the Butterfly: A Memoir of Life in Death* by Jean-Dominique Bauby, translated by
Jeremy Leggatt, translation copyright © 1997 by Alfred A. Knopf, a division of Penguin Random House LLC. Used by permission of
Alfred A. Knopf, an imprint of the Knopf Doubleday Publishing Group, a division of Penguin Random House LLC. All rights reserved.

Cross, Doris. Image courtesy of the estate of Doris Cross. Photograph by Alex Marks, courtesy of Marfa Book Company.

Gold, Mike. Image used by permission of Mike Gold.

Nussbaum, Daniel. Excerpts from *PL8SPK*. Published by HarperCollins, 1993. Used by permission of Daniel Nussbaum.

The map of the USA on page 44 is distorted according to Frederic Cassidy's own map
of the country, as seen in his *Dictionary of American Regional English*.

While every effort has been made to obtain permission to reprint copyrighted materials, there may be cases where we have been
unable to track a copyright holder. The publisher will be happy to correct any omission in future printings.

First edition 2020

Library of Congress Catalog Card Number pending
ISBN 978-0-7636-9066-3

20 21 22 23 24 25 CCP 10 9 8 7 6 5 4 3 2 1

Printed in Shenzhen, Guangdong, China

This book was typeset in Filosofia.
The illustrations were done in watercolor, gouache, and mixed media.

Candlewick Studio
an imprint of Candlewick Press
99 Dover Street
Somerville, Massachusetts 02144

www.candlewickstudio.com

ALPHAMANIACS

BUILDERS

of

26

Wonders

of the

WORD

PAUL
FLEISCHMAN

ART BY
MELISSA
SWEET

CANDLEWICK STUDIO
an imprint of Candlewick Press

CONTENTS

THE INVITATION

STEP INTO THE TENT ONE & ALL!

Take a seat,
remove your hats,

and discard as well your fear of the **outrageous,** the **brain-baffling,** the **bizarre.** Prepare to behold a pageant without equal. Perhaps you've seen fire-eaters and contortionists. But who among you has looked upon a lipogram? A mondegreen? Zaum?

For most of us, a tree is a tree. But some—the imaginers, the tinkerers—turn trees into canoes and their leaves into sails. Those you're about to meet are of this ilk. Their voyages? Extraordinary. Their persistence? Superhuman. The realm they explored? Not the physical one, but the airy land of letters.

You and I may barely notice the words flitting around us. But these men and women? Intoxicated by their shapes and sounds! Seeing music and mathematics where we see simply information! Collecting, dissecting, constructing verbal wonders as colossal and rarely glimpsed as the overgrown pyramids of the Mayans! Each of their tales is more astounding than the last. And every one of them true!

We take pride in our progress from caves to condominiums, but is that the whole story of humanity? If so, how to explain our elaborate pursuits that don't improve the roofs over our heads or add a cent to our bank accounts? Could it be that we live not on bread alone but also on curiosity, challenge, beauty, and play? Ponder the figures I'll now introduce. **Let the parade begin!**

Daniel Nussbaum

1949—

MASTER OF PL8SPK

Painters use paint, am I right? I would have been, until they looked back at centuries' worth of collage art and began adding strips of wallpaper and snippets from newspapers to their work. These days, museum walls routinely hold everyday objects, from postcards to dolls' heads. Who needs the art supply store? Artists increasingly find their materials in daily life.

Our first subject has done the same with words. Words picked from perhaps the strangest source ever tapped.

His name? Daniel Nussbaum!

His source? The letters and numbers on California's vanity license plates!

Yes, you heard me correctly. Confirmation can be found in his book *PL8SPK*. Combing a printout of the state's 1.3 million vanity plates, adding only punctuation, he retold well-known stories of every sort, beginning with the book of Genesis:

INTHE BEGINNG DYD GODCR8 HEAVEN PLUS EARTH. THE HLYSPRT CRUZD ONE TOTALEE VOID MONDO DARKNIS. THENN GODSAYD, "LET THERR BELITE." THERE WUZ LITE. THELITE IS CALLED DAY, THEDARK IZZ NIGHTT. GODZRAD. HESED, "XZLNT, FERSUR."

One gentleman, I see, has already left us. He'll miss the creation of the rest of the universe. Not to mention the automotive translation of the tragedy of Oedipus, the king of Thebes, who unknowingly killed his father and married his own mother. It begins:

ONCEPON ATIME LONGAGO IN THEBES IMKING. OEDIPUS DAKING. LVMYMRS. LVMYKDS. THEBENS THINK OEDDY ISCOOL. NOPROBS. OKAY MAYBE THEREZZ 1LITL1.

And then there's the myth of Narcissus: BHOLD MMOI!
Hamlet: 2BORWAT?
The Emperor's New Clothes: MYMYMY IMSOGQ.
The story of Noah's Ark: THEGR81 DOTH TEL NOAH, "IMFEDUP 2DMAAX."

Romeo and Juliet: GESSWAT! BE4 HEE SPLIT, ROMEO KISTME! HESSOQT! BYGTME! ISWEAR!

And, most appropriately given its celebration of driving, Jack Kerouac's novel *On the Road*, the word-jazz classic of the Beat era starring the restless Dean Moriarty:

HEYDIG! DIGDAT. DIGTHS. DIGGIN ITALL, THERZ DEANNME, ALLAUS YOUNG1S, EGCITED BY WOWLIFE, WANTING EVRYTNG ATONCE4 WEHAD2 MUCH2DO 2TASTE TOHEAR 2DIG2 SEEEE.

Is there a Californian in the house? You, madam? If you'd consider buying a personalized plate, you might be giving Mr. Nussbaum the very word he needs in the future.

You would? XZLNT!

Jean-Dominique Bauby

1952–1997

EYE WRITING

Authors are said to compose in studies and garrets. But some write in rooms no larger than their heads, producing no sound of quill or keyboard, their labor invisible to the world. Behold the incredible Jean-Dominique Bauby!

A man of culture and wit, he was the editor of the French fashion magazine *Elle.* Picture him driving a new BMW through Paris on a day in December. Then imagine his view out the window beginning to blur. He notices sweat beading on his forehead. Then he begins seeing double. He pulls to the curb.

When he gets out, he finds he's lost control of his muscles. He struggles to remain standing. He's rushed to a clinic. He tries to speak but can't. He remembers he has theater tickets for that night. His last thought is that he needs to call and cancel. Then he sinks into a coma.

Bauby has suffered a rare stroke to the brain stem. Twenty days later, he wakes from the coma. Gradually his mind regains its sprightly form. But his body? Immobile, an insect in amber. From head to toe, he's unable to move a muscle, save one. He can blink his left eyelid.

The doctors call his condition locked-in syndrome. Bauby is in solitary confinement within his own body. The sense of isolation is crushing, especially for a writer. But his ability to blink holds hope. The staff proposes using the alphabet to smuggle out his thoughts. He blinks his agreement.

In his head, he begins composing. He assembles words into sentences. He builds these into paragraphs and commits them to memory. Then a secretary recites the alphabet, the letters rearranged according to how commonly they're used in French: *e, s, a, r, i, n, t* . . . When Bauby hears the desired letter, he blinks. The letter is written down and the alphabet is recited again. Slowly, his report appears, his quick mind impatient with the painstaking process.

Meticulous people never go wrong: they scrupulously note down each letter and never seek to unravel the mystery of a sentence before it is complete. Nor would they dream of completing a single word for you. Unwilling to chance the smallest error, they will never take it upon themselves to provide the "room" that follows "mush," the "ic" that follows "atom," or the "nable" without which neither "intermi" nor "abomi" can exist.

He sketches life in the hospital on the English Channel that's become his new home.

In one section are a score of comatose patients, patients at death's door, plunged into endless night. They never leave their rooms. Yet everyone knows they are there, and they weigh strangely on our collective awareness, almost like a guilty conscience.

Staff and friends take their August vacations, then return. Outside, time flies. In room 119, it crawls.

Sunday. I dread Sunday, for if I am unlucky enough to have no visitors, there will be nothing at all to break the dreary passage of the hours. No physical therapist, no speech

pathologist, no shrink. Sunday is a long stretch of desert, its

only oasis a sponge bath even more perfunctory than usual.

He returns to the day of the stroke.

Our farewells were brief, our lips scarcely brushing together.

I am already running down stairs that smell of floor polish.

It will be the last of the smells of my past.

He gains the ability to move his neck slightly. He likens his body
to a heavy diving bell.

A very black fly settles on my nose. I waggle my head to

unseat him. He digs in. Olympic wrestling is child's play

compared to this.

Speech therapy is no easier.

On good days, between coughing fits, I muster enough

energy and wind to be able to puff out one or two phonemes.

On my birthday, Sandrine managed to get me to pronounce

the whole alphabet more or less intelligibly. I could not have
had a better present. It was as if those twenty-six letters had
been wrenched from the void; my own hoarse voice seemed
to emanate from a far-off country.

He's fed by a tube in his arm but dines more pleasurably on imaginary meals.

Depending on my mood, I treat myself to a dozen snails, a
plate of Alsatian sausage with sauerkraut, and a bottle of
late-vintage Gewürztraminer. . . . But today I could almost
be content with a good old proletarian hard sausage trussed
in netting and suspended permanently from the ceiling in
some corner of my head.

He'd been a world traveler. This doesn't change.

My mind takes flight like a butterfly. There is so much
to do. You can wander off in space or in time, set out for
Tierra del Fuego or for King Midas's court. You can visit
the woman you love, slide down beside her and stroke her
still-sleeping face.

What began as a letter to friends grows into a book. Its title is *The Diving Bell and the Butterfly*.

> *I am fond of my alphabet letters. At night, when it is a little too dark and the only sign of life is the small red spot in the center of the television screen, vowels and consonants dance for me.*

The book was published in 1997. Bauby died two days later.

Thomas Urquhart

1611–1660

THE WORDAHOLIC

Set your watches back five hundred years. Modern English is just crawling out of the chrysalis of Middle English. Modern French, Spanish, German, Italian are likewise emerging. An educated European must know Greek, Latin, Hebrew, and at least three of the new languages. The result? A call for a universal tongue, bridging Europe's many borders.

Latin is the most likely candidate, but too few speak it. Ancient Greek and Hebrew lack modern vocabulary. The new European tongues? They're strictly national and fractured further into dialects.

In 1629, with no universal language in sight, the philosopher René Descartes proposes that someone build one from scratch. Here would be a chance for a perfectly regular grammar, free of exceptions. A tongue sensibly spelled and simple to learn. A frictionless machine for thought, like the language of mathematics.

Twenty-four years later, the first reply to Descartes' challenge arrives. Not a list of verbs and nouns, but a book called *Logopandecteision* that contains the sketch for a new language. The author? A Scotsman who's perhaps the English language's foremost word coiner. A phrase-spitting rapper 350 years before rap. A man so drunk on language it was a wonder he could walk. I give you Sir Thomas Urquhart!

It was he who first translated into English François Rabelais' sprawling Renaissance masterpiece, *Gargantua and Pantagruel.* Though the book was already straining at the seams, Urquhart didn't merely translate, but enlarged and embroidered, filling it with fresh waterfalls of words.

He loved verbal abundance and assumed his readers did as well. In his book *The Jewel,* he apologizes for the many rhetorical techniques he neglected to deploy, from palilogetic elucidations to parabolary allegories:

> *I could have inserted dialogisms, displaying their interrogatory*
> *part with communicatively psymatic and sustenative flourishes;*
> *or proleptically, with the refutative schemes of anticipation*
> *and subjection.*

Verbal cascades were his specialty. His ideal university would teach not only the arts and sciences but "vaulting, swimming, running, leaping, throwing the bar, playing at tennis, singing, and fingering of all manner of musical instruments, hawking, hunting, fowling, angling, shooting" and more.

In an Urquhart love scene, his characters' passion was eclipsed by the author's even greater urge to generate words:

> *Thus for a while their eloquence was mute and all they spoke was but with the eye and hand, yet so persuasively, by virtue of the intermutual unlimitedness of their visotactile sensation, that each part and portion of the persons of either was obvious to the sight and touch of the persons of both; the visuriency of either, by ushering the tacturiency of both, made the attrectation of both consequent to the inspection of either.*

I'll pause a moment so that our brains might not overheat.

But wait, you say. What about his universal language? Was the author of a passage like that the best candidate to come up with a simple, stripped-down tongue?

I'll summarize his vision of his language and let you judge.

Number of parts of speech? Twelve. Number of voices? Four. Number of moods? Seven. Number of tenses? Eleven. Nouns and

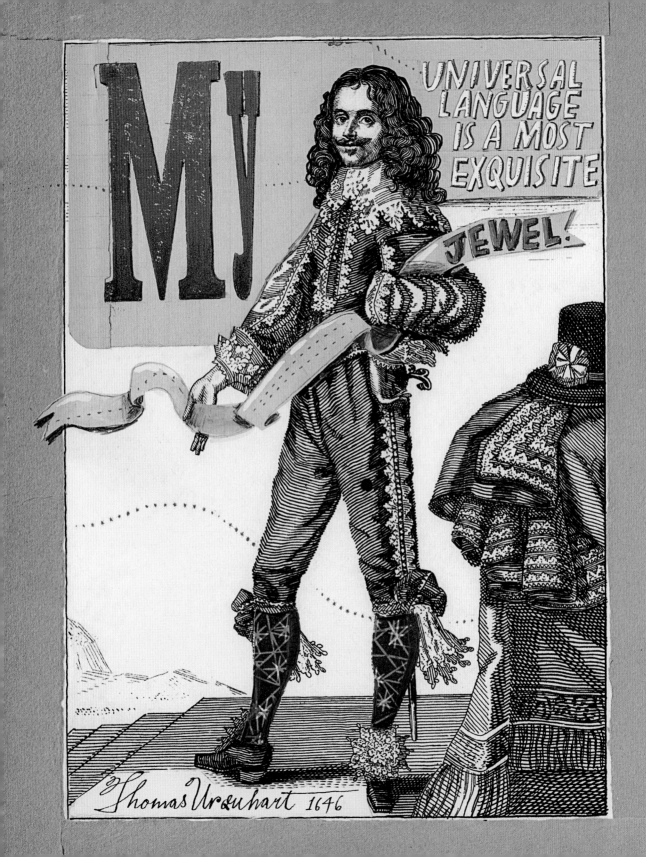

MY UNIVERSAL LANGUAGE IS A MOST EXQUISITE JEWEL!

Thomas Urquhart 1646

pronouns? Eleven cases and four numbers—singular, plural, dual, and redual. Number of genders? Eleven.

Additional features: Each word would have ten synonyms. Each letter would carry a meaning. Words could be read backward as well as forward. A single syllable would give us the year, month, day, hour, and minute. Numbers of any size could be expressed by a mere two letters.

His clinching claim? "The greatest wonder of all is that of all the languages in the world it is easiest to learn."

The lad before me looks doubtful.

"What about Descartes?" a woman asks.

By the time Urquhart's description was published, Descartes had died of pneumonia. An unnecessary visit by the angel of death, I'd say. Why? Because Urquhart's book would surely have accomplished the same end!

Jessie Little Doe Baird

1963–

THE RESCUER

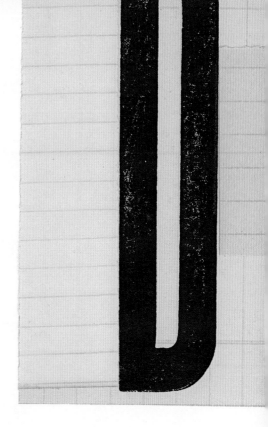

Healthy for hundreds or thousands of years, then a sudden decline. Status downgraded to threatened. Then endangered. Then the bell tolls: another extinction. I'm speaking not of a species but of a language.

When a plant or animal vanishes, we've lost not just the pleasure of its company but also its illuminating adaptations to its niche. The same is true with a language. We lose names for a place's geography and weather, fish and flowers. A unique way of describing time. Histories, prayers, proverbs, work songs. Jokes and stories. Millennia of accumulated wisdom on food and medicine that could be vital in fighting disease.

More than half of the world's seven thousand languages are expected to be gone by 2100, flickering out when their last speakers die or switch to other tongues. Can anything be done to halt this loss of linguistic diversity? Please welcome a woman who's bravely accepted the challenge. Three cheers for Jessie Little Doe Baird!

Four centuries back, her people, the Wampanoag, watched the Pilgrims land in Massachusetts. The Wampanoag still live there. But just as diseases tore through their villages, English overwhelmed their language, Wôpanâôt8âôk. By the middle 1800s, it was no longer to be heard.

Fast-forward to 1992. Baird, a Wampanoag working mother of four, begins having dreams featuring words she doesn't understand. She's sure she's being addressed by her ancestors. She realizes she's hearing Wôpanâôt8âôk.

A prophecy had predicted that the language would return. Baird sets out to bring that about. She's a social worker, not a linguist, but she's accepted into a program at the Massachusetts Institute of Technology. She earns a master's degree in linguistics. But how do you revive a language that has no living speakers?

She has an aid. A Puritan missionary worked with the Wampanoag, who rendered Wôpanâôt8âôk in writing and translated the Bible into it. This opens the door to the language's vocabulary and grammar. Working with an MIT professor specializing in indigenous languages, she compares Wôpanâôt8âôk with related Algonquian languages still being spoken.

When the language's outlines become clear, Baird faces an even greater challenge: teaching it to others. Wôpanâôt8âôk words can be a mouthful. But Baird is tireless. She founds the Wôpanâôt8âôk Language Reclamation Project. She teaches classes, organizes language immersion camps, writes curriculum and phrase books and stories in Wôpanâôt8âôk. With contributions from across the community of speakers, the Wôpanâôt8âôk dictionary climbs past eleven thousand words. Wampanoag children are learning to play Go Fish and Scrabble in their ancestors' tongue. A 2010 MacArthur grant recognizes the signal nature of her work: the first time a language with no native speakers has been revived in the United States.

There's a happy asterisk to that fact. In 2004 Baird's daughter Mae Alice is born. The first word she hears? *Kuweeqâhsun,* spoken by her mother. We would translate it as "good morning." Its literal meaning is "you are in the light." After a gap of seven generations, Wôpanâôt8âôk has its first native speaker.

"RECLAIMING OUR LANGUAGE IS ONE MEANS OF REPAIRING THE BROKEN CIRCLE OF CULTURAL LOSS AND PAIN.... THIS IS BUT ONE PATH WHICH KEEPS US CONNECTED TO OUR PEOPLE, THE EARTH, AND THE PHILOSOPHIES AND TRUTHS GIVEN TO US BY THE CREATOR."

--JESSIE LITTLE DOE BAIRD

Marc Okrand

1948–

HOW WOULD ALIENS TALK?

For his 1928 movie *The Wedding March,* director Erich von Stroheim re-created springtime Vienna in Hollywood, complete with thousands of fake apple blossoms made of wax and individually wired to tree branches. He insisted actors playing soldiers wear underwear monogrammed with the Austro-Hungarian coat of arms, just as actual soldiers would have, even though no moviegoer would see this.

Artists, like gods, create worlds. Some of them can't stop. Writers have littered their novels with the titles of made-up books, worked out detailed biographies of those books' authors, and even written complete reviews of their works.

Others go a step further by making these dreamworlds real. The writer Kurt Vonnegut invented the writer Kilgore Trout, who wrote the invented book *Venus on the Half-Shell*—which was then written by the science-fiction author Philip José Farmer. In his novel *The Abortion,* Richard Brautigan invented a library stocked only with unpublished manuscripts donated by their authors, a library later made real by a flesh-and-blood librarian and visitable today in Vancouver, Washington.

But few cases of extreme invention rival that of my next guest. Please shout out a hearty *majQa'* and prepare to meet Marc Okrand, the inventor of Klingon!

I refer, of course, to the language spoken by the ruthless race of ridge-heads in *Star Trek.* In the original TV series they spoke perfect English, as if they'd just walked in off Sunset Boulevard. Perhaps that's why they got a makeover in *Star Trek: The Motion Picture,* complete with a few words of gibberish. Two movies later the creators decided to furnish their world at a new level of detail and create more lines in a consistent Klingon tongue. They hired Marc Okrand.

His mission: to put together a gruff language befitting warriors. One that was alien-sounding, since the Klingons were extraterrestrial, but capable of being pronounced by actors.

Okrand put his PhD in linguistics to work. Pushing a shopping cart through the languages of the world, he put in lots of harsh sounds made in the back of the throat and threw in the *tlh* sound from the West Coast Native American languages he'd spent years studying. Unlike French, in which words are joined into a smoothly flowing stream, Klingon needed to sound rough and choppy, the reason Okrand seasoned it heavily with glottal stops—the sound that breaks up *uh-oh.* To make it sound alien, he mixed sounds rarely found in the same human language.

He furthered that alien quality in its grammar. English is termed an SVO language, its sentences usually in subject-verb-object order. Most of the world's languages put subjects first. Klingon? Object-verb-subject, the rarest pattern. Thomas Urquhart would have loved Klingon's myriad prefixes and suffixes that do surprising things, such as indicate the speaker's level of certainty in a statement. Outlandish? Turkish offers the same option.

If you want small talk and compliments, look elsewhere. The closest Klingon gets to *Hello* is *nuqneH,* meaning *What do you want?* But Okrand sprinkled in humor. Opponents of the English language's crazy spelling have noted that *fish* could reasonably be spelled *ghoti,* using *gh* as pronounced in *tough, o* as in *women,* and *ti* as in *nation.* The Klingon word for *fish* is *ghotI'.* Pain is *'oy'.*

You'd hear a lot of *oy*s from a class in Klingon. It's considered among the very hardest of languages to learn. Okrand only needed enough of it for *Star Trek III* at first, but since the Klingons kept returning he found himself gradually filling out the language. It was then taken up by *Star Trek* fans, who took world-building to a whole new level.

"You have not experienced Shakespeare until you have read him in the original Klingon." Perhaps some of you recall the line from *Star Trek VI.* The Klingon Shakespeare Restoration Project made this fiction a fact by translating *Hamlet* "back" into Klingon, published in a side-by-side edition with the English. *Much Ado About Nothing* has likewise been restored.

The *Epic of Gilgamesh* has been put into Klingon. So has China's *Tao Te Ching*. Work is going forward on translating the Bible.

Charles Dickens's *A Christmas Carol* has been performed in Klingon. An opera dramatizing the Klingon creation myth has been staged—in Klingon, of course. In 2013, perhaps for the sake of audiences at these performances, the search engine Bing began offering translation into Klingon.

The Klingon Language Institute sprang into being, promoting the language through courses, a journal, discussions, and conferences. Thanks to this group, we know to be careful with the Klingon insult "Your mother has a smooth forehead." Through its website, we can buy greeting cards in Klingon expressing *Happy Birthday* and *When do we attack?*

Okrand built this imaginary road further. *The Klingon Dictionary* he compiled has sold more than three hundred thousand copies and

* YOUR MOTHER HAS A SMOOTH FOREHEAD!

been translated from English into German, Italian, Portuguese, and Czech. This was followed by audiotapes on conversational Klingon and Power Klingon, a collection of Klingon proverbs, and *Klingon for the Galactic Traveler,* which describes its development, idioms, and slang. He alone can add new words to the language, announced to the world at his much-anticipated appearances at Klingon Language Institute conferences.

You might get the impression that a whole nation of nerds speaks Klingon. Not so. The language is so demanding that it's estimated that only a few hundred can read and write it. Fluent speakers might number as few as thirty. So why on earth—or the planet Kronos, the Klingon homeland—bother with it?

Let me use the ice-cream-licking youngster in the third row by way of reply. Are you aware of the vitamins A, D, E, and K you're ingesting? No? How about riboflavin and pantothenic acid, so vital to your health? No again. Then why in the world do you eat the stuff?

"It tastes good."

Ah. So does concocting a language. J. R. R. Tolkien put forty years of pleasurable tinkering into creating an entire family of fictional languages before using them in *The Lord of the Rings.* The answer to those who scoff at art's seeming uselessness? Ice cream.

Ignatius Donnelly

1835–1901

When we look at an optical illusion our eyes alternate between the two images we see. Some people have the same experience with words. They see not only letters but numbers.

Assign the number 1 to *a*, 2 to *b*, and so on. Then start adding up the numbers in words. Prepare to be surprised.

All + vote = democracy

Not + same = different

Hide + listen = eavesdrop

People have been using this method to search for secret messages in the Bible for centuries. But that's not the only place they've looked. Which is why I now bring you Ignatius Donnelly!

ALL
+ VOTE
DEMOCRACY

25
62
87

1 2 3 4 5 6 7 8 9 10 11 12 13

A B C D E F G H I J K L M

14 15 16 17 18 19 20 21 22 23 24 25 26

N O P Q R S T U V W X Y Z

Not only a writer of speculative fiction. Not merely an ardent believer in the lost civilization of Atlantis. Not simply a Minnesota congressman. But a man who, in a literary debate that's still boiling, captivated the world with his claim built on numbers.

All acknowledge the plays of Shakespeare as among the greatest products of world literature. But there's a problem. How could a country lad of scant education write so knowledgeably about every topic and time and social class? The answer, according to some: he didn't.

The Klingon Language Institute claims Wil'yam Shex'pir was a Klingon dramatist who lived light-years away from London. Here on Earth, among the many who've been proposed as the plays' actual author is Francis Bacon, statesman, scientist, and Shakespeare's contemporary. Dashing onstage in this drama, Donnelly delivered a riveting message—that he'd found cryptograms in the plays that proved beyond doubt that they'd been written by Bacon!

Mr. Donnelly was a lawyer. Allow me to present his case, with you serving as jury.

"Can we hang him?"

Mr. Donnelly is already deceased. I'm sorry to disappoint you.

"What's a cryptogram?"

A secret message. A topic Bacon had written about, most notably a method called *omnia per omnia*. That's Latin for *anything through anything,* because any message can be spaced out and hidden in a text. *There's a fly upon the window just now* contains the message *Fly now* if you know where to look.

Donnelly set off looking. He began with every fifth word in Shakespeare's plays. He strung them together but got only gibberish. So he tried every tenth word. Then every twentieth. Every fiftieth. Every hundredth. No better luck.

He counted five, ten, fifty, and one hundred words from the tops of pages down and from the bottoms of pages up. Then forward from the beginnings of acts and scenes and backward from the ends of acts and scenes. The result? Pure nonsense. Then he had a thought.

What would the secret message likely say? Probably, he reasoned, something along the lines of "I, Francis Bacon, son of Nicholas Bacon, wrote these plays." Suddenly, he knew what words to look out for.

In *Henry IV, Part 1,* the word *bacon* appears. "Bacon-fed knaves." An insult. Later on, the word *Francis* crops up. Donnelly felt sure they were linked, but how?

He noticed that *bacon* is the 371st word on that page. The man was a champion counter. He then realized that 371 is divisible by the page number, 53, yielding seven. A coincidence? Seven led him to several other key numbers, which in turn led him to the word *Nicholas* farther down, then to *son*, then *bacons*, then *Francis*.

"What's the message?"

It reads: "Bacon Nicholas son bacon's Francis."

"But the words are out of order."

True, and yet the sense is there, don't you agree? Donnelly certainly did.

"But the page numbers would be different in different editions. And then he wouldn't get seven."

True enough.

"And what stopped him from saying a number is important just so he could use it to pick out words that served him?"

If I can speak for him, I believe he'd tell you that his system was rigorously logical. By counting forward, and occasionally backward, using sometimes one column and sometimes both, the placement of vital words pointed him toward the crucial numbers 318, 371, 648, 594, and 477. From these, he derived what he called root numbers: 505, 506, 513, 516, and 523. Next he uncovered the multipliers: 10, 7, 11, and 18. Then the modifiers: 218 and 219, 197 and 198, and 30 and 50.

It's all described in detail in his book, *The Great Cryptogram*. Perhaps you'd like to work your way through its 998 pages and share his trembling awe when he stared at the message he finally uncovered: "Shak'st spur never writ a word of them."

Allow me to show you a page of his calculations.

And take thou this (O thoughts of men accurs'd)
"Past, and to Come, seemes best; things Present worst.
Mow. Shall we go draw our numbers, and set on?
Hast. We are Times subiects, and Time bids, be gon.

Actus Secundus. Scœna Prima.

Enter Hostesse, with two Officers Fang, and Snare.

Hostesse. M'. *Fang*, haue you entred the Action?
Fang. It is enter'd.
Hostesse. Where's your Yeoman? Is it a lusty yeoman
Will he stand to it?
Fang. Sirrah, where's *Snare?*
Hostesse. I, I, good M. *Snare.*
Snare. Heere, heere.
Fang. Snare, we must Arrest Sir *Iohn Falstaffe.*
Host. I good M. *Snare,* I haue enter'd him, and all.
Sn. It may chance cost some of vs our liues: he will stab.
Hostesse. Alas the day: take heed of him: he stabd me
in mine owne house, and that most beastly: he cares not
what mischeefe he doth, if his weapon be out. Hee will
foyne like any diuell, he will spare neither man, woman,
nor childe.
Fang. If I can close with him, I care not for his thrust.
Hostesse. No, nor I neither: Ile be at your elbow.
Fang. If I but fist him once: if he come but within my
Vice.
Host. I am vndone with his going: I warrant he is an
infinitiue thing vpon my score. Good M. *Fang,* hold him
sure: good M. *Snare* let him not scape, he comes continu-
antly to Py-Corner (sauing your manhoods) to buy a sad-
dle, and hee is indited to dinner to the Lubbars head in
Lombardstreet, to M. *Smoothes* the Silkman. I pra'ye, since
my Exion is enter'd, and my Case so openly knowne to the
world, let him be brought in to his answer: A 100 Marke
is a long one, for a poore lone woman to beare: & I haue
borne, and borne, and borne, and haue bin fub'd off, and
fub'd off, from this day to that day, that it is a shame to
be thought on. There is no honesty in such dealing, vnles
a woman should be made an Asse and a Beast, to beare e-
uery Knaues wrong.

Enter Falstaffe and Bardolfe.
Yonder he comes, and that arrant Malmesey-Nose *Bar-
dolfe* with him. Do your Offices, do your offices: M. *Fang,*
& M. *Snare,* do me, do me, do me your Offices.
Fal. How now? whose Mare's dead? what's the matter?
Fang. Sir *Iohn,* I arrest you, at the suit of Mist. *Quickly.*
Falst. Away Varlets, draw *Bardolfe:* Cut me off the
Villaines head: throw the Queane in the Channel.
Host. Throw me in the channele? Ile throw thee there.
Wilt thou? wilt thou thou bastardly rogue? Murder, mur-
der, O thou Hony-suckle villaine, wilt thou kill Gods of-
ficers, and the Kings? O thou hony-seed Rogue, thou art
a honyseed, a Man-queller, and a woman-queller.
Falst. Keep them off, *Bardolfe. Fang* A rescu, a rescu.
Host. Good people bring a rescu. Thou wilt not thou
wilt not? Do, do thou Rogue: Do thou Hempseed.
Page. Away you Scullion, you Rampallian, you Fusti-
larian: Ile tucke your Catastrophe.
Enter Ch. Iustice.
Iust. What's the matter? Keepe the Peace here, hoa.
Host. Good my Lord be good to mee. I beseech you
stand to me.
Ch. Iust. How now sir *Iohn?* What are you brauling here?
Doth this become your place, your time, and businesse?
You should haue bene well on your way to Yorke.
Stand from him Fellow; wherefore hang'st vpon him?

Host. Oh my most worshipfull Lord, and't please your
Grace, I am a poore widdow of Eastcheap, and he is arre-
sted at my suit.
Ch. Iust. For what summe?
Host. It is more then for some (my Lord) it is for all, all
I haue, he hath eaten me out of house and home: he hath
put all my substance into that fat belly of his: but I will
haue some of it out againe, or I will ride thee o Nights,
like the Mare.
Falst. I thinke I am as like to ride the Mare, if I haue
any vantage of ground, to get vp.
Ch. Iust. How comes this, Sir *Iohn?* Fy, what a man of
good temper would endure this tempest of exclamation?
Are you not asham'd to inforce a poore Widdowe to so
rough a course, to come by hir owne?
Falst. What is the grosse summe that I owe thee?
Host. Marry (if thou wert an honest man) thy selfe, &
the mony too. Thou didst sweare to mee vpon a parcell-
gilt Goblet, sitting in my Dolphin-chamber at the round
table, by a sea-cole fire, on Wednesday in Whitson week,
when the Prince broke thy head for lik'ning him to a singing man of Windsor; Thou didst sweare to me then (as I
was washing thy wound) to marry me, and make me my
Lady thy wife. Canst thou deny it? Did not goodwife *Keech*
the Butchers wife come in then, and call me gossip *Quickly?* comming in to borrow a messe of Vinegar: telling vs,
she had a good dish of Prawnes: whereby y didst desire to
eat some: whereby I told thee they were ill for a greene
wound? And didst not thou (when she was gone downe
staires) desire me to be no more so familiar with such poore
people, saying, that ere long they should call me Madam?
And did'st y not kisse me, and bid mee fetch thee 30.s. I
put thee now to thy Book-oath, deny it if thou canst againe?
Fal. My Lord, this is a poore mad soule: and she sayes
vp & downe the town, that her eldest son is like you. She
hath bin in good case, & the truth is, pouerty hath distra-
cted her: but for these foolish Officers, I beseech you, I
may haue redresse against them.
Iust. Sir *Iohn,* sir *Iohn,* I am well acquainted with your
maner of wrenching the true cause, the false way. It is not
a confident brow, nor the throng of wordes, that come
with such (more then impudent) sawcines from you, can
thrust me from a leuell consideration, I know you ha pra-
ctis'd vpon the easie-yeelding spirit of this woman.
Host. Yes in troth my Lord.
Iust. Prethee peace: pay her the debt you owe her, and
vnpay the villany you haue done her: the one you may do
with sterling mony, & the other with currant repentance.
Fal. My Lord, I will not vndergo this sneape without
reply. You call honorable Boldnes, impudent Sawcinesse:
If a man wil curt'sie, and say nothing, he is vertuous: No,
my Lord (your humble dutie remembred) I will not be your
sutor. I say to you, I desire deliu'rance from these Officers
being vpon hasty employment in the Kings Affaires.
Iust. You speake, as hauing power to do wrong: But
answer in the effect of your Reputation, and satisfie the
poore woman.
Falst. Come hither Hostesse.
Enter M. Gower.
Ch. Iust. Now Master *Gower;* What newes?
Gow. The King (my Lord) and *Henrie* Prince of Wales
Are neere at hand: The rest the Paper telles.
Falst. As I am a Gentleman.
Host. Nay, you said so before.
Fal. As I am a Gentleman. Come, no more words of it.
Host. By this Heauenly ground I tread on, I must be
faine to pawne both my Plate, and the Tapistry of my di-
ning Chambers.

"Rubbish."

I won't deny there were scoffers. Indeed, one of them used Donnelly's own system and uncovered the words "Will I am Shak'st Spur writ this play." Another went through *Hamlet* and detected this hidden message: "Don nill he the author politician and mountebanke will worke out the secret of this play." A cryptogram apparently placed in the drama 230 years before Mr. Donnelly was born.

"Congressman, is he? Won't get my vote."

As I mentioned, he's deceased.

"Rubbish. Let's hang him."

Ross Eckler

1927—2016

It's time now that you meet Ross Eckler, the longtime editor of *Word Ways: The Journal of Recreational Linguistics*.

Unfamiliar with such a pastime? If you're thinking of a game like Hangman, think again. Mr. Eckler's crowd goes in for extreme word-play. Extremely extreme.

Take the game of finding what they call shift pairs. Allow me to use *add* as an example. If you move each letter forward in the alphabet one place, the *a* becomes *b* and the *d*'s become *e*'s, changing the word from *add* to *bee*.

A —> B   D —> E   D —> E

A nice trick. Now who's got a word that works when you shift it two places?

No one? Then I'll give a word, courtesy of Mr. Eckler's book, *Making the Alphabet Dance. Ice* becomes *keg.* How about three steps? *Elm* to *hop.* Anyone for a four-stepper? *Paw* to *tea.* Notice how the *w* in *paw* becomes an *a?* It's fine to cross *z.* Just think of the alphabet as a circle.

Eight steps? *Log* to *two.*

Thirteen steps? *Ant* to *nag.*

Is it possible to extend the shift to a trio of words? Indeed it is. *Nun, tat,* and *bib.*

Maybe you think three-letter words are too easy. Likewise words of four and five letters. What about shift pairs with six letters? Mr. Eckler is ready with *fusion* and *layout.* Six letters *and* six places.

Seven letters? These are the longest shift pairs known in English, with only three found to date, among them *unfiber* and *bumpily.*

Granted, *unfiber* isn't terribly common. I haven't used the word myself in several days. So let's look for shift pairs that make some sort of sense. *Yes* and *oui,* obviously, but are there others?

Bet and *fix. Cubed* and *melon.* Or, for when an oil tanker goes aground, *errs* and *reef.* And notice the unlucky step size there. Thirteen!

But enough of all that. Let's play a new game. Instead of imagining the alphabet as circular, let's think about rearranging it. Consider the word *abet*. Notice that its letters appear in alphabetical order. Not uncommon with two- and three-letter words, but stunningly rare with longer ones. Indeed, of all the four-letter words in English, excluding those with repeating letters, a mere sixty words are in alphabetical order. But perhaps you've wondered: Couldn't we reorder the alphabet to make this easier?

Mr. Eckler and company have had the same thought. Indeed, they've discovered that remodeling the alphabet so that it reads BSFPWCHJQMOAVUIRNGLKTDZEXY will give us nearly four hundred such words. Imagine a world in which Spandex is alphabetical as well as stretchy. Wouldn't that be paradise!

It wouldn't? Well, then, what if we wanted to make it *harder* to produce words in alphabetical order? In that case you'd want the letters to play musical chairs again and sit down as follows: UIAOEYSDBPMHTGNLRKCFWVJQXZ. With that arrangement, only a single word of four or more different letters would come out in alphabetical order, the all but unknown word *iaos*.

Who would like to put *iaos* and *unfiber* together in a sentence?

I see that a woman in the back has fainted at the thought. Let's revive her with a stimulating search for isograms—words that have only one of each of the letters they contain. Short ones are easy. Each word in that last sentence is an isogram. But finding longer words is tougher, unless you're a *Word Ways* subscriber.

Eleven letters? *Documentary.* Twelve? *Housewarming.* Thirteen? *Troublemaking.* Fourteen? *Ambidextrously.*

Here in Mr. Eckler's book there's even a fifteen-letter one: *uncopyrightable.* If place names are allowed, *South Cambridge, NY,* has sixteen different letters.

But what about people's names that are isograms? Searchable telephone directories have made the hunt easier. The longest iso-gramatic name in the United States? *Melvin Schwarzkopf.* Seventeen letters.

But wait! Are we going to give up the quest at seventeen, when a score of twenty-six is possible? What about names that people don't have but *might* have? Mr. Eckler's playmates have thought of this, climbing their way to eighteen, then nineteen, then twenty, and finally to twenty-one letters with the following name: Emily Jung Schwartzkopf.

If such a dream woman were to exist, I feel sure she'd love to play with self-enumerating sentences. You know, a sentence such as "This sentence contains five words." Or "This sentence contains thirty-six letters."

Simple enough until you try enumerating other things. One *Word*

Ways reader came up with "In this sentence there are sixteen words, eighty-one letters, one hyphen, four commas, and one period." No easy feat, actually. Indeed, another contributor had to invent his own computer program in order to construct the following marvel:

> *This sentence contains three a's, three c's, two d's, twenty-six e's, five f's, three g's, eight h's, thirteen i's, two l's, sixteen n's, nine o's, six r's, twenty-seven s's, twenty-two t's, two u's, five v's, eight w's, four x's, five y's, and only one z.*

Perfection, in a peculiar way. A sentence that tells us absolutely nothing about the world beyond its borders!

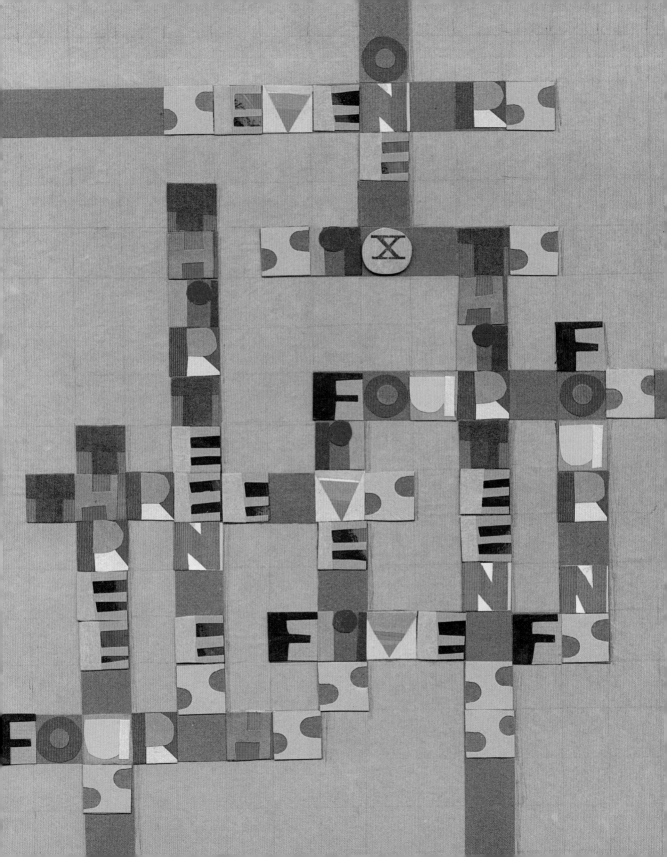

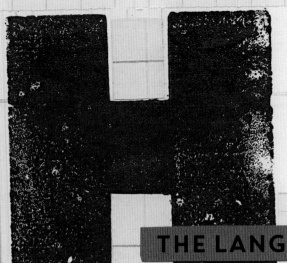

Frederic Cassidy
1907–2000

The many-headed Hydra that no one could slay? Killed by Hercules.

The all-devouring Minotaur? Laid low by Theseus.

Let us now sing the name of another hero who seemed not to know the meaning of the word *impossible.* Frederic Cassidy!

A Wisconsin professor who spent his early years in Jamaica, Cassidy grew up hearing French and English and their intriguing dialects around him. Just as a billiard player puts a spin on the cue ball, so does every speaker with language. Cassidy's life came to be dominated by a daunting quest — capturing the uncountable variations in American English, from coast to coast to coast and everywhere in between.

I see furrowed brows. Why bother? you ask. For the same reason meteorologists measure rainfall and demographers track popula-tion: to know what's going on. Lexicographers—writers of diction-aries—live to find out what words people are using and what they mean when they use them.

But there's a problem. Language changes from place to place, like soil. I say *porch* but you might say *veranda*. Students of dialect like Cassidy rejoice in this. They're enraptured by the where of language, mad collectors of varied pronunciations, local terms, odd phrases. Not English as it's taught in school but as it's actually spoken, from the pulpit to the locker room to the Twitterverse.

To know your area's butterflies you need a butterfly net. But how to catch a language?

In the 1870s, linguist Georg Wenker tried to get a fix on German in all its variety. He spent ten years writing fifty thousand letters to German schoolteachers, asking them to render the same forty sen-tences in their local dialect.

Or, instead of having the language come to you, you can go to it. Such was the method of Frenchman Edmond Edmont, who toured his country from 1896 to 1900 on a bicycle to collect the material for the *Linguistic Atlas of France.*

The problem in America? Too many miles! Studies had been made of New England and other regions, but no one had thrown a net over the whole country. Until Cassidy.

First he secured funding for the project. Then he chose one thousand communities to be surveyed, from big cities to tiny crossroads, covering all fifty states. He refined a questionnaire designed to elicit terms from every corner of life, from pie-making to politics. He gathered eighty data collectors, taught them how to administer the questionnaire, and told them to choose only informants who'd lived virtually all their lives in their communities. In 1965, his researchers loaded supplies into their campers, dubbed Word Wagons, and set off. They were on the road for five years.

Every place they stopped, they asked the same questions, including:

What do you call the jewelry that goes around a woman's forearm?

Speaking of a light rain that doesn't last, you'd say it's just a _____.

What nicknames are used around here for beer?

What joking names do you have for a doctor?

What do you open up and hold over your head when it rains?

I can see you wondering how many questions were asked. One thousand eight hundred and forty-seven. So many that it usually took several informants to cover them all. On top of this, fieldworkers collected newspapers and diaries and other specimens of local printed language.

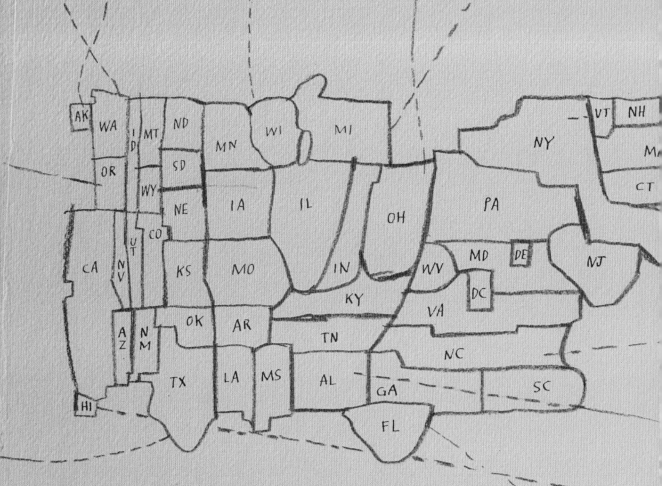

QUESTION:
WHAT OTHER NAMES DO
YOU HAVE AROUND HERE
FOR THE DRAGONFLY?

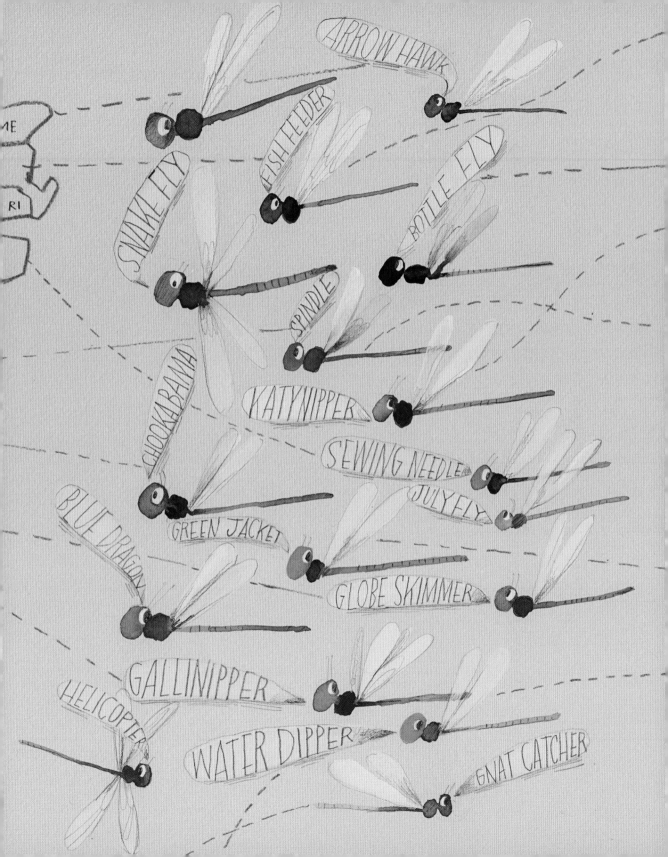

Pronunciation? Captured with tape recorders. Each informant was taped speaking freely for twenty minutes. They were also recorded reading "Arthur the Rat," a story devised for its spectrum of sounds.

Does five years seem like a long time? It was only the beginning. The collectors came back with so much material that it took decades to analyze it. Cassidy found seventy-nine different variations on *dragonfly,* from *snake doctor* to *ear cutter,* and 176 terms for dust under a bed. Just as biologists map plants' and animals' ranges, researchers showed the prevalence of *all-ee all-ee in free, buttermilk sky,* terms for *grandmother,* and nearly three thousand other words and phrases on U.S. maps redrawn to reflect linguistic factors.

Questionnaires, recordings, newspapers, maps. I trust that no one will cry out in shock when I reveal that the first volume of the *Dictionary of American Regional English* didn't see the light of day until fifteen years after the field-workers returned, that it weighed in at a healthy 1,056 pages — and that it covered only the letters *A* through *C.* Three more volumes were published over the next seventeen years. Finally, in 2012, volume five, *SL to Z,* appeared, forty-seven years after the Word Wagons set out and twelve years after Cassidy died.

What's that you say?

"Probably asking his questions in the next life."

Indeed. And he probably thought to bring pen and paper to write down the answers.

Doris Cross

1907–1994

THE WORD SUBTRACTOR

"Language is a city to the building of which every human being brought a stone." So wrote the American man of letters Ralph Waldo Emerson.

My next notable turned this notion upside down, bringing forth her creations not by piling up stones but by taking them away. I give you Doris Cross!

Serendipity—finding something wonderful by accident—is as crucial to artists as bread. It can strike anytime, anywhere. For Cross, serendipity arrived in a dictionary.

It was the 1960s. The dictionary was old, a 1913 *Webster's*. As an aid to users, printed boldly at the top were the left page's first word

so that
of the earth
vessel

where

Arms

anchor

A female anchoret.

in seclusion

the world

like fishes of
the Mediterranean, used for pickling or making a sauce

classic.

su

us

headed double
Two-edged

and

join word with word, clause with clause

sentence

to

sentence with

come go.

when

I was

a little
an-dan'te

flowing

Bearing
cluster

staminate

pistillate

Homer's " Iliad "

Ἀνδρομάχη]

was rescued

an'dro

and

A man-headed sphinx.

ἀνήρ, ἀνδρός,

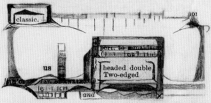

See STORY.

and the right page's last. The book was open to the *L*'s. The two words at the top were *laceration* and *lamb.* Cross stared at the pair. They were joined by pure chance, yet seemed possibly to hold some secret meaning. In that moment of wonder, not one but two new art forms were born—erasure art and altered books.

Cross was trained as a painter and began acting out a librarian's nightmare. She crossed out words. She painted over parts of pages. She colored what had been black and white. The words she left visible expressed thoughts that the dictionary's writers never foresaw.

Prose became poetry. Pairings appeared that might never otherwise have occurred to anyone. A book that seemed frozen was suddenly wriggling with new messages—not purposely hidden like those Ignatius Donnelly sought, but noticed and excavated by a reader.

The idea must have been in the air. Later in the decade, the British artist Tom Phillips did the same thing with an obscure 1892 novel called *A Human Document.* Where the words *together* or *altogether* appeared, he covered over all but *toge* and turned the book into a beautifully ornamented work called *A Humument* about the character Bill Toge.

Using found materials wasn't new. The Dadaists of the early 1900s cut up newspapers and made poems from the words and phrases that fell to the floor. The notion has fueled a century of projects since, from the Pulitzer Remix sponsored by *The Found Poetry Review,* in which poets build new poems from phrases in the novels crowned with the Pulitzer Prize for fiction, to Annie Dillard's collection *Mornings Like This,* in which each poem rearranges lines from a different source, from medical textbooks to Vincent van Gogh's letters.

Doris Cross stuck to a single source. Many of her followers have done the same, with brain-boggling results. Janet Holmes took *The Poems of Emily Dickinson* and subtracted it into *The ms of m y kin* — *ms* being the abbreviation for *manuscript* — recasting poems written during the Civil War into poems about our era's soldiers fighting in Afghanistan and Iraq. Poet Ronald Johnson turned John Milton's *Paradise Lost* into *Radi Os.* Jen Bervin transformed Shakespeare's sonnets into *Nets.* Erasure has been applied to everything from *How to Prune Fruit Trees* to *The 9/11 Commission Report.*

Doris Cross's makeover of the dictionary likewise helped inspire the altered book movement. Artists began adding flaps and folds, cutting out shapes, sewing in objects, and reengineering bindings, playing with possibilities in flabbergasting fashion. They're still doing so.

The moral? It's not only the alphabet that can dance, but meaning, and the paper it's written on. We salute you, Doris Cross!

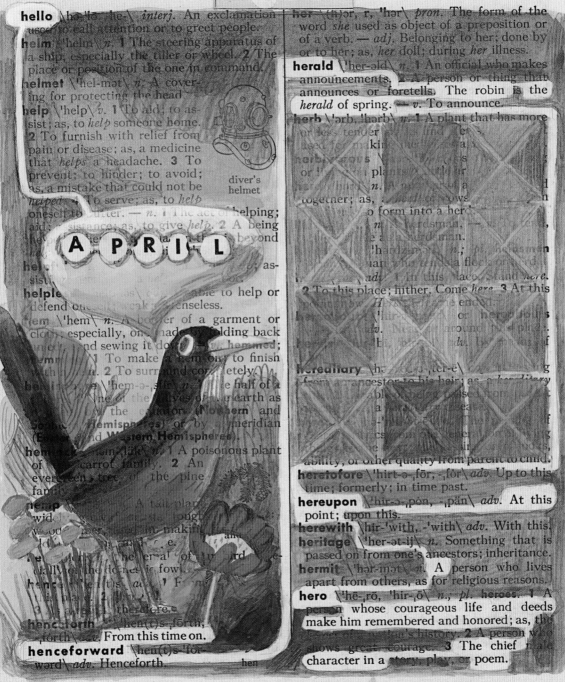

hello \he-lō, he-\ *interj.* An exclamation used to call attention or to greet people.

helm \'helm\ *n.* **1** The steering apparatus of a ship, especially the tiller or wheel. **2** The place or position of the one in command.

helmet \'hel-mət\ *n.* A covering for protecting the head.

help \'help\ *v.* **1** To aid; to assist; as, to *help* someone home. **2** To furnish with relief from pain or disease; as, a medicine that *helps* a headache. **3** To prevent; to hinder; to avoid; as, a mistake that could not be *helped*. **4** To serve; as, to *help* oneself to butter. — *n.* **1** The act of helping; aid; assistance; as, to give *help*. **2** A being or thing that helps; ... beyond help ... as, ... helpless ... able to help or defend oneself; weak; senseless.

hem \'hem\ *n.* A border of a garment or cloth, especially, one made by folding back the edge and sewing it down; as, hemmed; ... **1** To make a hem on; to finish with ... *n.* **2** To surround completely.

diver's helmet

A P R I L

hemi- ... half of a ... the halves of ... earth as ... the equator. (Northern and Southern Hemispheres) or by a meridian (Eastern and Western Hemispheres).

hemlock \'hem-,läk\ *n.* **1** A poisonous plant of the carrot family. **2** An evergreen tree of the pine family.

hemp ... A tall plant ... wid ... wood ... in making ...

... the er-al of ... bird ... cially of the tones of fowl.

... henceforth ... \'hen(t)s-,fȯrth, -fȯrth\ *adv.* From this time on.

henceforward \'hen(t)s-'fȯr-wərd\ *adv.* Henceforth.

her \(h)ər, r, 'hər\ *pron.* The form of the word *she* used as object of a preposition or of a verb. — *adj.* Belonging to her; done by or to her; as, *her* doll; during *her* illness.

herald \'her-əld\ *n.* **1** An official who makes announcements. **2** A person or thing that announces or foretells. The robin is the *herald* of spring. — *v.* To announce.

herb \'ərb, 'hərb\ *n.* **1** A plant that has more or less tender ... used for makin ...

herbivorous ... or ... pla ... — *n.* ... together; as, ... o form into a herd ... n. ... ردsman ... *n.* ... man who tends a floc ... — *adv.* **1** In this place. Stand *here*. **2** To this place; hither. Come *here*. **3** At this ...

her ... \'hir- ... or ... *adv.* Near ... around th ... place ... b ... n. ... hangs ...

hereditary \hə- ... -ter-ē\ ... from ... ancestor to his heir; as, a hereditary ... ability, or other quality from parent to child.

heretofore \'hirt-ə-,fōr, -,fȯr\ *adv.* Up to this time; formerly; in time past.

hereupon \,hir-ə-'pän, -'pȯn\ *adv.* At this point; upon this.

herewith \hir-'with, -'with\ *adv.* With this.

heritage \'her-ət-ij\ *n.* Something that is passed on from one's ancestors; inheritance.

hermit \'hər-mət\ *n.* A person who lives apart from others, as for religious reasons.

hero \'hē-,rō, 'hir-,ō\ *n.*, *pl.* **heroes.** **1** A person whose courageous life and deeds make him remembered and honored; as, the ... history. **2** A person who shows great courage. **3** The chief male character in a story, play, or poem.

Robert Shields

1918–2007

THE DIARIST WHO INCLUDED EVERYTHING

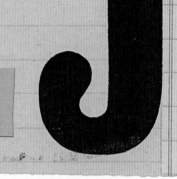

I hold two books. Am I going to juggle for you? In a manner of speaking. Along with delivering some background information, I'll read from this dictionary of quotations in my left hand and recite as well from the volume in my right, which contains excerpts from the diary written by the astonishing Robert Shields. Let's begin with one of his typical mornings.

Porch temperature 45°. Porch floor temperature 40°.
Study temperature 77°.

"I am a camera with its shutter open."
— CHRISTOPHER ISHERWOOD

10:00-10:05 I groomed my hair with a scrub brush.

Shields grew up in Indiana. His father was a champion speed-typist who reached 222 words a minute. On an ancient manual machine, mind you.

> **10:05-10:10** I fed the cat with tinned cat food.

Shields worked as a minister and high school English teacher. After retiring he began keeping a diary. He decided not to leave anything out.

> **10:10-10:20** I dressed in black Haband trousers, a pastel blue Bon Marché shirt, the blue Haband blazer with simulated silver buttons, both hearing aids, eyeglasses, and the 14° Masonic ring.

> *"No man was ever written down but by himself."*
> — SAMUEL JOHNSON

> **10:20-10:25** I tried to pick a spot of Krazy Glue off my black trousers that got on them yesterday. I was unsuccessful. Maybe it was Friday that I spotted them. I put a dab of liquid black shoe polish on the blemish and it helped some.

He and his wife lived in Dayton, Washington. He usually described his days in five-minute increments. At night he awoke every two hours to jot down his dreams.

> **10:45** Grace and I left the house.

"The desire to write grows with writing."
—DESIDERIUS ERASMUS

```
10:48 [Odometer:] 97182.0 We left the post office after
dispatching mail. It was 62°.
```

"Writing is busy idleness."
—JOHANN WOLFGANG VON GOETHE

He recorded what he ate. His pulse. His blood pressure. Every visit to the bathroom. His phone calls. His reading. His junk mail.

```
10:55 [Odometer:] 97187.1 We passed the entrance to
Lewis and Clark Trail State Park.
```

After a while he was typing hours every day. Some years he'd produce over three million words. Afraid his IBM Wheelwriter would break, he had six backup Wheelwriters and rotated among them.

```
11:23 [Odometer:] 97207.8. The Prime Cut Restaurant,
1760 Isaacs.
```

He typed in two columns on 11-by-14-inch sheets. Onto the paper he taped receipts, restaurant menus, and other physical documentation.

```
11:29 I ordered a breaded fish filet and a baked potato,
and Grace ordered a shish kebab. The fish was $1.99 and the
shish kebab was $2.99.
```

Monday, January 31, 1994 Dayton, Washington

3:35-4:05 Klara called. Well, I am getting to
be a celebrity in my own right. I am no different
from anybody else. I keep a diary. Thousands keep
a diary. Mine just happens to be longer than
anybody else's.

6:30-6:35 I put in the oven two Stouffer's
macaroni and cheese at 350°.

6:35-6:50 I was at the keyboard of the
IBM Wheelwriter making entries fo

6.5

Spider
Specimen

7.3

8:1

Whe

10:

hou

> "It's gotten to the point
> that if I don't write it
> down, it's as if it never
> happened."
> --Robert Shields

Tue

12.

IBM Wheelwriter making entries for the diary.
1:49 We left the Safeway parking lot in the plaza.
sunny and brite.

When a stroke put him in the hospital, he took notes by hand. His output dropped to a million words a year.

> **12:25–12:30** I stripped to my thermals. I failed to mention that the Tri City Herald weighed in this morning at 1 lb., 11½ ounces.

A second stroke robbed him of the ability to type. After twenty-four years, he had no choice but to stop. He'd bound his typed pages into ledgers, then packed the ledgers in large cartons. It took ninety-one of them to hold his diary. He donated it to Washington State University in 1999, stipulating that it not be read for fifty years.

The most renowned diary in English was kept by the politician Samuel Pepys, a detailed look at London life in the 1660s that ran to more than a million words. Two twentieth-century American diarists exceeded fifteen million words. Shields's work contains more than thirty-seven million words. It's the longest known diary in human history.

"This is no book," wrote the poet Walt Whitman. "Who touches this touches a man."

Sven Jacobson

1922–

MISSPELLINGS "R" HIM

Next up, Sven Jacobson! A man whose work proves the adage that you don't know your home country until you travel abroad. Or your home language.

Why should that be? Because we cease to notice what we're surrounded by. A foreign visitor to the United States, by contrast, sees Groundhog Day and college football and breakfast burritos as strange and worthy of study. Sven Jacobson is just such a tourist, a professor at Sweden's Uppsala University who's made a career of studying English.

He's examined our preverbal adverbs. What are those? I haven't the foggiest. We use English without knowing how it works. But Mr. Jacobson knows.

He's scrutinized our word order. He's probed the distinctive vocabulary of the Boy Scouts. He's deduced the complicated rules that govern where in a sentence we place the word *probably*. But when it comes to noticing the unnoticed and then examining it in detail, Mr. Jacobson set a mark for the ages when he published his study entitled *Unorthodox Spelling in American Trademarks*.

You recall the poem by Elizabeth Barrett Browning that begins "How do I love thee? Let me count the ways"? This is precisely what Mr. Jacobson has done, revealing not only our deep love of intentional misspelling when it comes to brands and businesses, but the myriad ways we accomplish it. No phoneme or grapheme—sounds and letters to you and me—is safe from our fiddling. Allow me to display a few of his finds along with their categories.

Bit-O-Honey: deletion of consonant phoneme

Lectric Shave: deletion of vowel phoneme

Neva-Lose: spelling based on regional pronunciation

Briter'n Ever: deletion of vowel phoneme

Tuf-Grip: simplified, phonetic spelling

Tru-Blu: reduction of aphthongal graphemes

Aire-Flo: increased number of vocalic graphemes

Wright Temp: increased number of consonantal graphemes

Ye Olde Shoppe: imitation of earlier orthographic usage

Thun Thoot: imitation of children's lisped *s*'s

Can't-*B*-Lost: spelling based on letter names

Restinbed: word boundary omission

Takacheck: omission of aphthongal *e* in the first syllable

Betr Kake: simplification of intersyllabic double consonantals

There's more. Much more. A very great deal more.

The work was published in 1966. One can only imagine Mr. Jacobson's thrill when he later set eyes on Blu-ray or Mortal Kombat. When he listened to will.i.am while munching on Cheez-Its. When he used Reddit or Flickr or Tumblr. When he arranged a ride via Lyft.

None of those, however, probably matched the excitement of that day in October of 1994. What happened then? Toys "R" Us opened its first store in Sweden.

Mike Gold

1953–

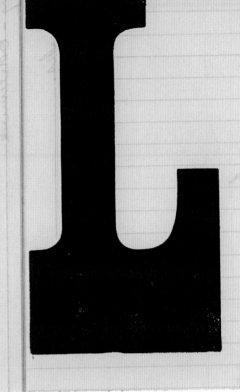

HOW MANY WAYS CAN YOU WRITE A?

Pick a word, any word, as a magician might say.

Most of us see only its meaning. The poets and musicians will notice its sound: the scrape of consonants, the river of rhythm. But language possesses another quality that only a few are attuned to. I'm speaking of its purely visual side, the realm of ascenders and descenders, x-heights and serifs, slants and swashes. Which is why I've invited the amazing Mike Gold! A man who's devoted himself to the look of letters in eye-popping, mind-staggering fashion.

Why do so? The impulse is ancient. The Romans of old spent centuries refining the proportions of their letters, adding nothing at all to their meaning but producing an alphabet still revered for its beauty.

APEX

COUNTER

CROSSBAR

SERIF

CAP HEIGHT

X-HEIGHT

SANS SERIF

BASELINE

Today's type designers and writers of calligraphy carry the work forward. What, asks the young lady, is *calligraphy*? The word is Greek for "beautiful writing." Accomplished with pens and inks, the very art Mr. Gold has given himself to.

We think of artists as solitary. But humans are social creatures, and even artists know the pleasures of working together. In 1990 Mr. Gold joined a group of calligraphers who came to be known as Scribes 8. They evolved a remarkable tradition. They would meet and decide on a theme for a joint project. Each would spend months creating eight copies of his or her component. At their next meeting they'd assemble the finished pieces into a book or a box or a portfolio of artwork—one for each member—and then decide on the next project.

To create is to solve problem after problem. If no solutions are in sight, an artist must invent them. How does one strengthen that brainstorming muscle? The calligrapher Larry Brady suggested coming up with one hundred variations on a single letter.

Scribes 8 heard about this and decided to turn it into a project. They would each produce one hundred *a*'s, that vital leader of the alphabet. They would then each invite a writer to contribute a short celebration of the first letter and would combine the results into a book.

The idea behind the hundred variations was that the first fifty letters would exhaust the mind of its usual answers, forcing it to enter unexplored territory. Mr. Gold accumulated fifty, pushed into the unknown, and crossed the hundredth-letter finish line.

Perhaps you've accomplished something you weren't sure you could do and then noticed yourself wanting to do it again. Success can be addictive. After his first hundred, Mr. Gold wanted to keep going. He reached two hundred. Then three hundred.

How many ways could a person form two uprights and a cross-bar? Or the crouching lowercase *a*? Pen or marker or brush in hand, Mr. Gold filled tiny notebooks with *a*'s. New ideas rained down and sprouted up. Some opened doors onto new corridors and wings, each room marked *A*. Months after starting, he made it to five hundred. Then six hundred. Then seven hundred. Then eight hundred.

The calligraphers picked out their favorite *a*'s. The essays came in from the writers, who included the children's author Paul Fleischman. Anyone here heard of him? I thought not.

The book was titled *A Book,* published in 1997 in a single edition of one thousand copies. Twenty years later, Mr. Gold is still at it. Between the many he's tossed and those he's kept, he estimates he's made over one thousand *a*'s. Yes indeed, applause is most definitely in order. What a testament to the boundlessness of human imagination! Allow me to show you the slimmest sampling of Mr. Gold's *a*'s:

Toss out meaning, and all that's left of language is shape and sound. And yet letters themselves have meaning for us. *A* has been described as intimidating, pompous, bold, cold. Some people feel strongly that *a* is red. Letters seem to have their own secret lives.

I leave you with the words of the Swedish writer Olof Lagercrantz: "Every letter is endowed with a wealth of association, reawakens memories, gives rise to hopes, and is, seen in the right light, a complete little poem."

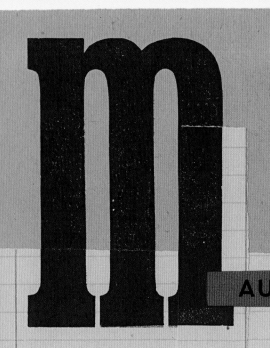

David Wallace
1928—2017

Sherlock Holmes discovered who did it by close attention to objects: clothing, cigar ash, the location of a callus on a hand. Can words be read the same way?

There may be no bloodcurdling screams, but there are unsolved mysteries aplenty in the world of words, along with prowling detectives. Today I've brought you one of them, a man who tackled one of our most celebrated conundrums and gave us a tool that's still prying open cases, with startling results. Please make welcome David Wallace!

For over two hundred years, there's been a hole in American history. The issue: Who wrote the Federalist Papers? You remember them from your seventh-grade history class. Essays signed only by "Publius" that promoted the adoption of the nation's new Constitution. The hole isn't a tiny one, as they were penned by some of the country's Founding Fathers—James Madison, Alexander Hamilton, and John Jay. But who wrote what?

There are eighty-five papers in all, with nearly all the authors known. But both Madison and Hamilton later claimed to have written twelve of them. How to decide?

In 1851, an English mathematician had an idea that might help. Count the number of letters in a sample of an author's work and divide by the number of words. A writer's average word length, he believed, would be absolutely distinctive. Dickens's was calculated to be 4.34 letters.

Unfortunately, it was found that different writers had nearly identical averages. Fortunately, this method had led to no arrests or hangings. But was there a key still waiting to be found?

There was, though it would take a century to find it. Enter David Wallace in the 1960s. And his colleague, Frederick Mosteller. And a tool Sherlock Holmes never had: an IBM computer, something thought of at the time as useful mainly for numbers. Wallace and Mosteller thought differently.

They fed the Federalist Papers into the computer at the Massachusetts Institute of Technology. Instead of word length or unusual terms that might serve as flags, they'd decided to pay

Holmesian attention to everyday words that earlier sleuths had ignored. They programmed the computer to check thirty of them.

The results appeared. Lo and behold, Hamilton turned out to use *upon* ten times more often than Madison. Madison used *by* much more often than Hamilton did. The words Wallace and Mosteller had chosen painted two distinct literary profiles. The twelve disputed essays? All Madison's, they believed, a view that still prevails. But that's only the beginning of the story.

Their breakthrough launched a new field called *stylometry,* which applies statistical analysis to literary style. In the years after Wallace and Mosteller published their findings in 1964, their methods have been refined and applied to other authorial mysteries. Did Saint Paul write all of his Epistles? It's thought not. Did L. Frank Baum write *The Royal Book of Oz*? No again. Did General George Pickett, famed for his charge at Gettysburg, write the Civil War letters published under his name? I'm afraid I must report that stylometry indicates that they were in fact the work of his wife.

In the midst of the 1996 presidential campaign, an election novel appeared that starred a character much like Bill Clinton. Its author was given only as Anonymous. The book became the talk of the nation. Who was the writer? Then an English professor found quirks of style that pointed strongly to *Newsweek* reporter Joe Klein. Klein denied the charge repeatedly, then later confessed.

A similar drama played out in 2013 with the crime novel *The Cuckoo's Calling.* The author, listed as Robert Galbraith, was unusually knowledgeable about women's clothing. Stylometry and an insider tip pointed the finger at none other than J. K. Rowling. She confessed, revealing that she'd used the pseudonym so as to be judged by her writing, not her name.

Stylometry has been used on suicide notes, on online postings, on extortion letters. What about Shakespeare and Bacon? you ask.

Most scholars today think Shakespeare indeed wrote his plays. Bacon still has his followers, as do the Earl of Oxford and playwright Christopher Marlowe. With today's computers able to do far more than Wallace's, they've taken a major role in this drama. When researchers taught a computer to distinguish Shakespeare's work from Marlowe's, it put *Henry VI, Part 3* in the Marlowe column. And then came the news in 2015 that two stylometrists had added a new work to Shakespeare's canon: a drama called *Double Falsehood,* which they believe he cowrote with the playwright John Fletcher.

Today, though few of us know it, Wallace's work linking language and computers is woven into how search engines find results, how e-mail filters catch spam, and how Siri handles requests.

Excellent idea, madam. Ask Siri who wrote *Hamlet*!

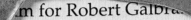

...m for Robert Galbr...

...Cuckoo's Calli...

...he waiting time by snapping the white canv...
...e road, the entrance to the tall red-brick a...
...t, and the balcony on the top floor from w...
...en.

...e tightly packed paparazzi stood white vans wi...
...te dishes on the roofs, and journalists talking, son...
...guages, while soundmen in headphones hovered. Bet...
...the reporters stamped their feet and warmed their...
...of coffee from the teeming café a few street...
...the woolly-hatted cameramen filmed th...
...rs, the balcony, the tent concealing the...
...mselves for wide shots that encompass...
...d inside the sedate and snowy Mayfa...
...black doors framed by white stone...
...bs. The entrance to number 18 was...
...als, some of them white-clothed forensic ex-
...be glimpsed in the hallway beyond.
...e television stations had already had the news for several
...Members of the public were crowding at either end of the
...held at bay by more police; some had come, on purpose, to
...others had paused on their way to work. Many held mobile

ROBERT
GALBRAITH

the
and
of
a
to
in
r
that
with
for
as
but
at
not
on
from
by
this
an
so
no
where
which
into
upon
like

AUTHOR CANDIDATES

J. K.
Rowling

Bohumil Hrabal

1914–1997

Our next subject is a gold-medal winner in a stadium empty of spectators, in an event few people know exists.

His sport? Not the marathon, but the marathon sentence.

Consider, for instance, William Faulkner's nearly 1,300-word sentence in his novel *Absalom, Absalom!* Figuring four hundred words to a page, that's a sentence stretching over three pages. Impressive, you think.

Running hard in the next lane is Ireland's James Joyce. There he is at work on his masterpiece *Ulysses,* finally placing a period at the tail of a sentence 4,391 words long, three times longer than Faulkner's. From impressive to unhinged, you say to yourself.

In the lane to his left, that's Jonathan Coe running for England. He, too, finally staggers across the finish line. His score? An incredible 13,955 words, for a sentence more than thirty pages long in his novel *The Rotters' Club*. From insanity to hostility toward readers, you think. Surely this is the end of the race.

But aim your binoculars at the last lane. Do you see him? A balding, solidly built scribe, trotting briskly? He smiles as he passes. His book? The novel *Dancing Lessons for the Advanced in Age,* published in 1964. Its subject? The trials of life and love, revealed through the comical autobiography an old man delivers to six sunbathing women. The author is one of the Czech Republic's most respected writers. His accomplishment: stuffing an entire novel of 128 pages into *a single sentence.* All hail Bohumil Hrabal!

The woman before me looks unwell. An English teacher, you say?

I hesitate therefore to mention that the book in fact *isn't* a sentence. For Hrabal didn't end it with a period, giving the book the added distinction of being most likely the longest sentence fragment ever written!

Yes, the medical tent is to the right. English teachers care so deeply, and sentence fragments are their sworn enemies. I wish her well. But as she probably goes hoarse from asking students to write slowly and carefully, it's probably for the best that she won't meet our next figure.

Corín Tellado

1927–2009

SPEED WRITER

I now bring you an entrant not in the marathon, or even the ultramarathon, but in a race that lasts an entire lifetime! The goal: to write more books than anyone else.

Those in this elite group likely regarded their activity less as a competition than a compulsion. There is indeed a condition known as hypergraphia, associated with epilepsy, which compels people to write diaries, lists, a repeated saying, a single word, or nonsense. The Russian novelist Dostoyevsky and the British writer Lewis Carroll may both have suffered from this disorder. More relevant here perhaps is typomania, an obsession with being published.

Consider the American writer Isaac Asimov, who typically typed ninety words a minute from seven thirty in the morning until ten at night. He published more than four hundred books on so many topics that he's said to be the only author whose works can be found in every major Dewey decimal classification.

And let us not forget Georges Simenon of Belgium, the author of more than five hundred mysteries, written in nine-day marathons, before and after which Simenon would weigh himself. No, I do not know why.

He in turn was topped by the British queen of romances, Barbara Cartland, who published more than seven hundred books. When an author dies, it's not unusual to find an unknown manuscript or two. In this author's case, an additional 160 novels were found.

And then there's Ryoki Inoue, a Brazilian surgeon whose passion for the American West led him to wear jeans and boots under his surgical gown. When he gave up the scalpel, he found he could write a Western in less than a week. Then in a single day. Then in a few hours. After ten years, he'd passed the one-thousand-book mark. He not only wore out keyboards but also required ten different publishers and twenty-plus pseudonyms to keep from competing with himself. When the document from the *Guinness Book of World Records* arrived, certifying his number one position, it was already fifteen works behind.

Inoue's current number of published books isn't clear. It may be that he's already been passed by another Brazilian, R. F. Lucchetti, who reached 1,547 titles in 2014.

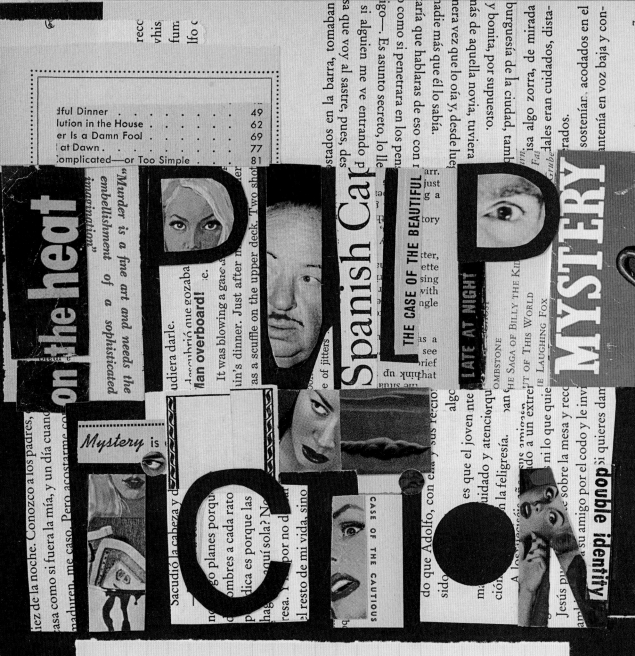

"Some months, the censors rejected four novels. **I TOLD THINGS CLEARLY.** Censorship taught me to imply things."

Corín Tellado

But all these contenders have been eclipsed by the daughter of a Spanish mechanic who wrote her first novel at age eighteen. All rise and acclaim Corín Tellado!

Her publisher so liked that first novel, a brief romance, that it paid her to write one a week, which she did for the next forty years. The dictatorship of Francisco Franco, who ruled Spain in this era, encouraged such escapist reading. When Tellado left her heroine blind at the end of one manuscript, her editor demanded, "Give her an operation." Her book tally would be higher if censors hadn't rejected stories containing women driving cars and pursuing ends other than pleasing fathers and husbands.

She branched out into an early form of graphic novel. After Franco died, she wove abortion and rape into her books and even published erotica. She's said to be the most-read Spanish author after Miguel de Cervantes, who wrote *Don Quixote.* Her total after starting work at five a.m. for sixty-three years? More than four thousand novels!

It's lonely at the top. But at least you've got a lot to read.

Raymond Queneau

1903–1976

**THE BOOK THAT TAKES
A MILLION CENTURIES TO READ**

The man you'll now meet possesses the quirky quintessence of the letter q — Raymond Queneau! A Frenchman who was both an acclaimed writer of avant-garde fiction and a serious mathematician specializing in number theory. How to bridge this divide?

He did so in 1960 when he cofounded the group called Oulipo, a contraction of words meaning "workshop of potential literature." Its purpose? To study forgotten literary genres and invent new ones. To experiment with patterns borrowed from games and mathematics. To find inspiration not in freedom, but in rules and constraints.

What do its members do?

They write poems that read the same backward as forward.

They take a proverb's words and explore all possible word orders to see what messages turn up.

They try merging geometry and literature.

They write tautograms—texts in which all words start with the same letter.

They replace nouns in famous texts with their dictionary definitions. Or with the noun seven places down in the dictionary.

They write poems that rhyme according to the eye but not the ear.

BASTILLE DAY

For this best of all army parades

I obtained a seat in the façades

And the tears brought an ache

To my graying moustache

As I heard the tanks rumbling in Hades

But perhaps the most acclaimed Oulipo production, unveiled in 1961, was created by Queneau himself.

You've seen books for children with the pages cut into strips, each with a different animal part so that readers can make impossible beasts. That's what Queneau did. Except in this case, the possibilities are rather more extensive.

Instead of animals, Queneau used sonnets, a poetic form with fourteen lines. He wrote a set of ten. He ended each of the first lines with the same sound, so that any of his ten would work there without upsetting the rhyme scheme. Likewise with all the other lines. He gave them the same grammatical structure and similar subject matter, so that each of the sonnet's lines had ten interchangeable variants. Then he had them printed and cut into strips.

Queneau loved numbers. Let's do the math with him. Fourteen lines. Ten sonnets. Who here can tell us how many possible sonnets we could make?

Correct! Ten to the fourteenth power. What would that number look like?

Correct again! One followed by fourteen zeroes. The name for that number is one hundred trillion. Or, as expressed in Queneau's title, *One Hundred Thousand Billion Poems*.

Being a mathematician, he made some further calculations. If someone were to read one sonnet per minute for eight hours a day, two hundred days a year—leaving ample vacation time—how long, he wondered, would it take to read every poem in his ten-page book? The answer: *more than a million centuries!*

Preposterous, and yet true. I double-checked his math just an hour ago. What this means is that the sonnet you chance to read will more than likely never have been read before. Or be read again, in all the history of the world. To the delight of Oulipo's membership, the vast majority of the book's sonnets remain latent, waiting, potential . . .

IT ISN'T HAPPINESS I AM CONCERNED WITH BUT EXPERIENCE.

--RAYMOND QUENEAU

ONE HUNDRED THOUSAND BILLION POEMS

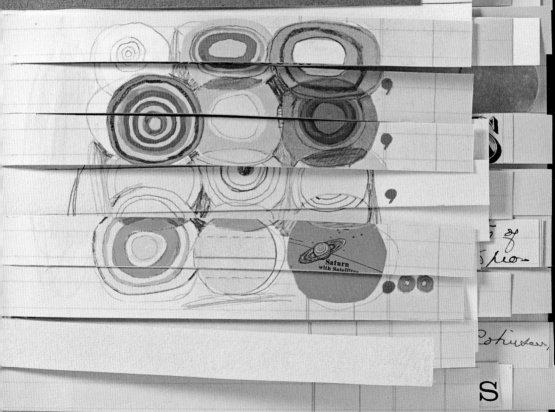

Saturn
with Satellites

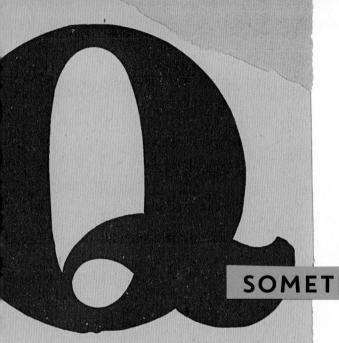

Georges Perec

1936–1982

SOMETHING'S MISSING

Seven years after Oulipo's founding, the group invited a new member to join. They chose well.

The man in question loved lists, games, and patterns. He wrote crossword puzzles for a French magazine. At the scientific library where he worked, he was known to type the text for catalog cards in triangles and other shapes. He would travel light-years beyond such projects in the years to come. Prepare to meet the astounding Georges Perec!

You've no doubt come across palindromes, strings of words that read backward as well as forward, such as "Madam, I'm Adam" or "A man, a plan, a canal—Panama." Eleven and twenty-one letters, respectively. For Oulipo's first published anthology, Perec contributed a palindrome of 5,556 letters.

He wrote a set of eleven poems, each with eleven verses and each built from only eleven letters, the total number of lines adding up to 1936, his birth year.

His novel *Life: A User's Manual* takes the knight's tour from chess—in which a knight moves so as to stop on every square just once—and uses it to visit each room of a Paris apartment block.

But Perec has a place in this parade for a work more befuddling than those. I speak of his novel that isn't simply a novel but the world's longest lipogram!

What's a lipogram? you ask.

A work that deliberately excludes a letter.

Why do such a thing?

Apparently it's human nature. Lipograms go back to the ancient Greeks. Perhaps some of you noticed that the first four letters of *lipogram* are the last four of *Oulipo*. It seemed a sign to the group that this was a constraint worth exploring.

For Perec, the idea of a novel-length lipogram was a challenge he couldn't resist. But what letter to leave out? A rarely used letter like *x* would make the game too easy. Perec went to the other extreme. He would leave out the letter *e*.

The most common letter in French! This would remove from his vocabulary the words for *I, the, of, not. Me* and *she. Can* and *can't. To do, to be, to say.*

An Everest of a quest! Perec set off, accompanied by Queneau and other Oulipo members, who contributed passages.

The story concerns the disappearance of a man named Anton Vowl. Those who try to find him disappear as well, a fate befalling anyone pronouncing the letter *e*. When a bartender is about to say the word *eggs*, which in French both contains and sounds like the forbidden letter, he explodes.

Perec aimed for a tone as natural as possible. The book begins:

> *Incurably insomniac, Anton Vowl turns on a light. According to his watch it's only 12:20. With a loud and languorous sigh Vowl sits up, stuffs a pillow at his back, draws his quilt up around his chin, picks up his whodunit and idly scans a paragraph or two.*

Perec so succeeded that at least one reviewer failed to notice the missing *e*'s. Did they notice as well that there's no chapter five? Perec left it out because *E* is the fifth letter of the alphabet.

The book was published in 1969 as *La Disparition*—"The Disappearance." To translate it into English was a task as daunting as writing it. As *disappearance* has *e*'s, the wily translator, Gilbert Adair, titled the book *A Void*.

That was the least of his challenges. Perec had stuck into the novel famous French poems he'd rewritten without *e*'s. Adair did the same with classics in English. Hamlet's "To be or not to be" soliloquy begins "Living, or not living: that is what I ask." Poe's famous raven became "Black Bird." Its famous refrain: "Not Again!"

The book was light, but not its origins. In French, *e* sounds just like the word *eux,* meaning "them." Perec's family were Polish Jews who'd come to Paris between the world wars. Perec's father enlisted in 1940 and promptly died. Paris fell to the Nazis. The four-year-old Perec was spirited out of the city to relatives in the unoccupied zone.

And his mother?

It's believed she was rounded up in Paris and killed at Auschwitz. Since no trace of her was found, no death certificate could be issued. While writing *La Disparition,* Perec had in his desk the government's pronouncement on the matter. The document was titled *Acte de Disparition.*

Can the dead return?

In literature they can. Perec's next book was *Les Revenentes* —"The Ghosts." It's an erotic novella overflowing with *e*'s. Indeed, it's a work, impossible though it may seem, in which the letter *e* is the *only* vowel used!

Its author disappeared from this earthly realm at age forty-five. But Oulipo still meets, occasionally publishing its members' work. Dying doesn't remove one from its rolls. Raymond Queneau and Georges Perec are still regarded as members in good standing.

NEVERMORE!
THE RAVEN BY EDGAR ALLAN POE
of western United States. Abbreviation, Nev.
nev′er (nĕv′ẽr), adv. Not ever; at no time.
nev′er·more′ (nĕv′ẽr·mōr′), adv. Never again.
nev′er·the·less′ (nĕv′ẽr·thẽ·lĕs′), adv. In spite of that; however.
new (nū), adj. 1. Having existed for a short
BLACK BIRD BY ANTON VOWL
NOT AGAIN!

Simon Vostre

1486–1521

Books once took years of labor by scribes to produce and were therefore worth their weight in rubies. Even early books printed on presses might feature painted illustrations and decorations in gold and silver leaf. How could such treasures be protected from careless readers? From forgetful borrowers? From outright thieves?

Anathema!

Thank you, but I didn't sneeze. An *anathema* was a pronouncement of banishment. A warning. A curse, often inscribed on the book's first or last page. A curious literary genre mixed from religion, fantasy, and the vivid description of horror novels. All the way from Paris, I bring you the early publisher of religious books, Simon Vostre—a master of the form!

Whoever steals this Book of Prayer

May he be ripped apart by swine,

His heart be splintered, this I swear,

And his body dragged along the Rhine.

O rapturous vision! A printer's love for his books rivals a mother's for her children. This thing of beauty was composed by Vostre in 1502. But he's not alone. In truth, he stands at the front of a long line of anathema writers going back centuries. Some appealed to readers' compassion:

If you do not know how to write you will consider it no hardship,
but if you want a detailed account of it let me tell you that the work
is heavy; it makes the eyes misty, bows the back, crushes the ribs
and belly, brings pain to the kidneys, and makes the body ache
all over.

Others relied on precise instructions:

Therefore, O reader, turn ye the leaves with care, keep your fingers
far from the text, for as a hail-storm devastates the fields, so does
the careless reader destroy the script and the book.

Eleanor Worcester

This BOOK IS MINE

AND I IT LOST,
AND YOU IT FIND.
I PRAY YOU
HEARTILY TO BE
SO KIND, THAT
YOU WILL TAKE
A LITTLE PAIN,
TO SEE MY BOOK.
BROUGHT HOME AGAIN.

{DO NOT DESTROY, IN ANY WAY
OR YOU WILL LIVE TO
RUE THE DAY! ✦◯}

✦ IN OTHER
WORDS,
IT'S CURSES .
. FOR YOU...

Multiple threats were always popular:

*If anyone take away this book, let him die the death; let him be
fried in a pan; let the falling sickness and fever seize him; let him
be broken on the wheel, and hanged. Amen.*

With only words to hold back negligence and theft, scribes had to
paint their imagined punishments in full color:

*For him that stealeth, or borroweth and returneth not, this book
from its owner, let it change into a serpent in his hand and rend
him. Let him be struck with palsy, & all his members blasted.
Let him languish in pain crying aloud for mercy, & let there be
no surcease till he sing in dissolution. Let bookworms gnaw his
entrails in token of the Worm that dieth not, & when at last he
goeth to his final punishment, let the flames of Hell consume
him forever.*

The tradition was alive long before the copyists of the Middle
Ages. In my local library I found this book you see in my hand, which
includes the following warning from none other than Ashurbanipal,
ancient king of Assyria, who was seriously concerned about his well-
ordered library of clay tablets:

I have arranged them in classes, I have revised them and I have placed them in my palace, that I, even I, the ruler who knoweth the light of Ashur, the king of the gods, may read them. Whosoever shall carry off this tablet, or shall inscribe his name on it, side by side with mine own, may Ashur and Belit overthrow him in wrath and anger, and may they destroy his name and posterity in the land.

The oldest known book curse, from twenty-six centuries in the past! We've come a long way from then.

Or have we? What's this I see at the back of my library book?

Should the borrower lose, damage, or fail to return the item, a replacement fee will be charged along with a $10 nonrefundable billing fee.

Not quite like having your body disassembled by wild pigs. Book curses just aren't what they used to be.

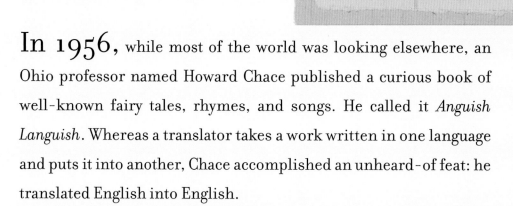

Howard Chace

1897–1982

FIRST SPEAKER OF ANGUISH LANGUISH

In 1956, while most of the world was looking elsewhere, an Ohio professor named Howard Chace published a curious book of well-known fairy tales, rhymes, and songs. He called it *Anguish Languish*. Whereas a translator takes a work written in one language and puts it into another, Chace accomplished an unheard-of feat: he translated English into English.

"How?" demands the woman before me.

By finding English words whose meanings were wrong but whose sounds approximated those of the right words. *Little Red Riding Hood* became *Ladle Rat Rotten Hut*. Here's how that story begins:

Wants pawn term dare worsted ladle gull hoe lift wetter murder
inner ladle cordage.

The entire tale is told in this manner, ending with the sage advice: "Yonder nor sorghum stenches shut ladle gulls stopper torque wet strainers."

What madman, you ask yourself, would do this? The sort, like Chace, who taught French and wanted to show his students that speaking a language requires knowing not only its grammar but its music. If you speak the words *wants pawn term* in a wooden monotone you'll leave your listeners baffled. But pause briefly after *wants,* then let your pitch fall on *term,* and suddenly it sounds like *once upon a time.* A brisk tempo helps. Try it with some of the other titles in his book:

Guilty Looks Enter Tree Beers

Marry Hatter Ladle Limb

Oiled Murder Harbored

Casing Adder Bet

Hormone Derange

Chace's book sent waves through the world of wordplay. It still does. Lincoln's Gettysburg Address was rewritten in his manner, retitled "Spaghettibird Headdress." Likewise Lewis Carroll's

anguish languish

by H. L. CHACE

LADLE RAT ROTTEN HUT
and the anomalous woof.

Here further verse thyme in book firm is the extraordinary version of LITTLE RED RIDING HOOD that Arthur Godfrey read aloud on his program — and made famous. And with it are more FURRY TELLS, NOISIER RAMS, FEY MOUSE TELLS, and THONGS, especially transcended by Prof. H. L. Chace, the originator of ANGUISH LANGUISH, for you, your friends, and your family to half pun wit.

(Continued on inside flaps . . .)

"Jabberwocky"—"Bean ware the jumbo wok, Mason"—nonsense phrases portraying a nonsense poem. Most appropriate!

This fun-house language came to be known as Anguish Languish. Its users then realized that the difficulty and reward could be raised by limiting the words they could use. Instead of the whole English language, Jay Ames re-created "Jack and Jill" solely from surnames in the Toronto phone book:

> *Jacques Aingell*
> *Wenn Opper Hill*
> *Topicha Paylor Watter*
> *Jacques Fell Down*
> *Ann Brooke Hiss Crown*
> *Angell Kamm Tumber Linn Affe Tarr.*

What about looking for the correct sounds in non-English languages? Luis van Rooten published a book of English Mother Goose rhymes recast entirely from French words, with *Humpty Dumpty* rendered *Un petit d'un petit*. John Hulme's book *Mörder Guss Reims* does the same with German words.

In the same dual-language tradition is Dog Latin, in which Latin words that make scant sense make the sounds needed to tell a tale in English:

Caesar adsum jam forte

Brutus aderat

Caesar sic in omnibus

Brutus sic in at

Caesar had some jam for tea

Brutus had a rat

Caesar sick in omnibus

Brutus sick in 'at

This verse goes back more than a century to English schools, where Latin was a standard subject. It makes more sense if you know that tea is an afternoon snack, an omnibus is a bus, and that you wear a 'at on your head. Was Dog Latin perhaps Mr. Chace's inspiration?

The tradition gained new life in our time with the beaming of pop music across borders. An English-language song like "Daddy Cool" could now be heard by Russians, for whom the chorus "What about it Daddy Cool?" sounded strangely close to the Russian words meaning "Barbara is frying chicken." This has given birth to a whole genre of YouTube videos called *soramimi*—Japanese for "misheard"—in which songs in other languages are given dubbing or subtitles, the new words similar in sound but wildly divergent in meaning.

Not that you have to cross languages for this. So many people heard guitar wizard Jimi Hendrix singing "Excuse me while I kiss the sky" as "Excuse me while I kiss this guy" that he began singing it that way as a joke.

This mishearing is common but lacked a name until the writer Sylvia Wright described childhood memories of listening to her mother read aloud the Scottish ballad "The Bonny Earl of Murray." Instead of "They hae slain the Earl of Murray and laid him on the green," she heard "They hae slain the Earl of Murray and Lady Mondegreen." Her essay on this drew so much notice that *mondegreen* now appears in dictionaries as the accepted term for a misheard word or phrase.

Silly trifles? So it might seem. But reflect a moment. Humans have been speaking for hundreds of thousands or possibly millions of years, but writing is a brash newcomer. How does it work? It uses symbols to stand for the sounds we say. When we make those sounds, out comes the word and its attendant meaning. Every book, in effect, is written in Anguish Languish.

As Howard Chace might say, *Ink ready bull!*

Robert McCormick
1880–1955

YOU MAY FIRE WEN REDY!

We've all heard people accept some outrage, from war to five a.m. garbage pickups, with "It's always been that way." But just because something is long-standing doesn't make it right. Or inevitable. A case in point is the misery caused by the English language's maddening, mystifying spelling.

We speak a Germanic language, written with a Roman alphabet that was adopted from the Greeks, who took it from the Phoenicians. No wonder we have problems! We have letters doubled to no effect. The same letters representing different sounds. Different letters representing the same sounds. Letters that convey no sound whatsoever. Bedlam!

ONE THOUSAND YEARS AGO

WEIRD

WAS SPELLED

WYRD

SO MUCH FOR "i BEFORE e."

Benjamin Franklin proposed ejecting six letters from the alphabet. Andrew Carnegie, Mark Twain, Theodore Roosevelt, the National Education Association—all called for change. Yet every attempt to remedy the situation went aground on the same rock: our attachment to the familiar.

"We insist," wrote the spelling reformer Thomas Lounsbury, "that all who come after us shall suffer as we have suffered; shall turn over the same pages already wet with our tears; shall tread the same paths which our worn and blistered feet have trodden before."

And then came a man who refused to perpetuate this woe. I bring you Robert Rutherford McCormick!

Most men lacked the means to put changes into practice. McCormick, by contrast, was the editor of the *Chicago Tribune,* the self-proclaimed "World's Greatest Newspaper." Other men hadn't the stomach to stay the course when complaints came in. But McCormick had been a colonel in World War I and had looked upon slaughter. The grandson of a spelling reformer, he'd been spoiling for this fight for years.

On the icy morning of January 28, 1934, the first shot was fired. In a front-page editorial, McCormick boldly announced that the *Tribune* would introduce twenty-four respellings starting that very day. These included *catalog, dialog, advertisment,* and *fantom.* On the sports page, readers should be prepared to see *hocky.*

He waited a month, then led another charge, ushering in *agast, burocrat, crum, pully,* and *missil.*

With irrational tradition on the run, McCormick's army advanced further, parading in print the words *rime, sherif,* and *staf,* then brazenly defying Merriam-Webster with *glamor, trafic,* and *jaz.*

Eighty respellings in two months! Chicagoans were reeling. Inconsistencies were pointed out. The writer H. L. Mencken described spelling reformers as "over-earnest and under-humorous men."

Savings in ink, paper, and labor, predicted to be great, turned out to be undetectable. Rather than joining the *Tribune* as hoped, other publications took potshots at it. After five years of warfare, the paper's own editors rebelled.

McCormick resisted. A cease-fire was reached. Half the respelled words were dropped.

But McCormick then launched an attack against *gh.* Presumably delighting Chicago's schoolchildren, *though* became *tho* and *through* became *thru.* McCormick then opened a major front against *ph* that resulted in *autograf, photograf,* and *telegraf.*

Teachers, who'd been counted on as allies, claimed the *Tribune* was confusing their students. The tide turned once more against McCormick. Under heavy bombardment from readers, he retreated on the word *sofomore.* Then *iland.*

Unbowed, he considered changing the spelling of his own name to *Micormak.* At the last moment, his wife stilled his hand.

1950. The *Tribune* sadly reports the death of playwright and spelling reformer George Bernard Shaw. His will funds a competition to design a new English alphabet in which each letter will correspond to a single sound. Five hundred submissions arrive. A winning script of forty-eight letters is chosen, but fails to catch on.

1953. A spelling reform bill successfully makes its way through the British House of Commons. It reaches the House of Lords, where it's voted down.

1955. McCormick dies. He's buried in his World War I uniform. A few months later, the *Tribune* gives up the fight. Word by word, the old spellings begin returning. *Thru* and *tho* survive until 1975. *Catalogue* and *dialogue,* the first to be cast out of the newspaper's pages, are the last to creep back in.

Eventually, *catalog* and *dialog* would be widely accepted and reappear in the *Tribune.* There were few such successes. Today, almost the only evidence of the spelling war is to be found on a few elevators at the *Tribune* plant—elevators marked FRATE.

Mary Ellen Solt

1920–2007

PAINTING WITH LETTERS

We love besting a challenge. And then making it tougher. Take the crossword puzzle, for example.

When crosswords spread from the United States to England in the 1920s, people found them too easy. So British puzzle makers added puns, rhymes, and anagrams to their clues. Edward Mathers's crosswords in the London *Observer* were so cruelly hard that he signed them with the name Torquemada, the first Grand Inquisitor of the Spanish Inquisition, notorious for torturing his victims. England mourned when Mathers died, having been happily tortured by him for years.

Poets are no different. Not just any word will do. Rhyme schemes and rhythmic patterns make poetry much harder to write than if meaning were the only consideration. When patternless free verse became fashionable, Robert Frost complained that "Writing free verse is like playing tennis with the net down."

But some poets have felt that even rhythm and rhyme don't offer enough obstacles. Raising the net higher, they demand of themselves poems that also *look like their subjects.* All hail the writers of concrete poetry!

The stage would barely be big enough for them all. Simmias of Rhodes would win the award for farthest traveled—all the way from fourth-century BCE Greece. He's said to have begun the tradition with a poem about the two-bladed ax used to build the wooden horse that brought the Greeks inside the walls of Troy—a poem in the shape of an ax blade.

Pattern poetry of this sort has popped up throughout the centuries. The seventeenth-century English poet George Herbert produced poems in the shape of an altar and bird wings, possibly the first concrete poetry in English. And let's not forget Lewis Carroll, who included in *Alice's Adventures in Wonderland* a poem in the shape of a mouse's tail, its font getting progressively smaller toward the tip.

There have been poems in the shape of bells and bottles, a maze, a trombone, a swan and its reflection, an hourglass, a lute, the key to a 1954 Dodge. Still too easy, you say? Let's raise the bar further! Consider the *calligrammes* of the Frenchman Guillaume Apollinaire, tackling subjects never before attempted, including city scenes of buildings, bridges, and rivers made of words.

If we keep going down this word-painting path, where do we end up? In the mesmerizing, eye-enchanting realm of my next subject, the remarkable Mary Ellen Solt! A scholar and practitioner of concrete poetry who took it nearly to abstraction. A poet who worked closely with typesetters and exhibited her work in museums. Her 1966 bouquet of floral poems, *Flowers in Concrete,* is one of the most dazzling celebrations of the visual side of language ever produced. Let your eye inhale "Zinnia."

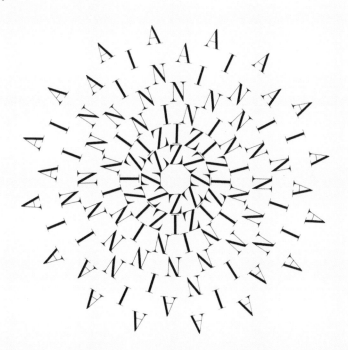

Are there any among you who don't come away revived by its beauty and buzzing with possibility?

I feel the same.

CLOUDYowhhangingclouAUTUMNL SWELTING sapphireblue-greAazued*with*pinkyellowgreyCCOU
ppppiiiiiinnkkkkK
Sapphire-BLUEazureberylandultrmaineunderGREYBLUEdarkLININGovercerulеanbl
urpleLAVENDERFOGHEARINGkoAUTUMNCRICKETbeginsummerisgonesummerisgonethebi
ummerraspberasboraywaytosumacsorberiaPPPPIIIIIII NNNNNNKKKKKKVIOLETRLUE
lightmagentsbecomeindigo BLUEluminouslimosfadingtosepia PINKPINKROSE
FUCHSIAAZALEA ROUGE
GREYgrey skybluepinkpopsicle
bluishy

B R
b A
r a M
mm
B L
l E S
b e
l
s

zz zzZz Zzzzzzzzzzzz
z

B

zzzz zzzzz

BRAMBLES

A. A. Morrison
1911–1998

No sooner do colonists step off their ships than they begin speaking differently from how they did back home. England and America have been described as two countries divided by a common language. In one, you go to the store to buy Popsicles, potato chips, and cookies; in the other, ice lollies, crisps, and bickies. Pronunciations likewise head down different paths.

This phenomenon played out strikingly in Australia. Visitors to the new nation soon began noticing that the colonists' English vowels had apparently melted in the heat. This divergence continued for nearly two hundred years, until an Australian writer had a momentous realization. He and his countrymen were no longer speaking English.

His name? A. A. Morrison.

The language actually being spoken around him? Strine.

Say the word a few times. Recall any examples of Australian accents you've heard and you'll see that *Strine* is an approximation of the word *Australian* as it's pronounced Down Under.

How did this great discovery come about? Morrison said he read about a British author approached by an Australian book buyer at an autographing.

"Emma Chisit," said the customer, putting forth the book.

The author inscribed the name inside, not realizing that the buyer was actually inquiring about the book's price.

This scene revealed to Morrison the existence of the previously unreported Strine. He donned the pen name Afferbeck Lauder, Strine for "alphabetical order." He donned as well the title of Professor of Strine Studies at the University of Sinny—Strine for the nation's largest city, Sydney—and began publishing his findings in the *Sydney Morning Herald.* In 1965, they were gathered into his book *Let Stalk Strine.* A few examples:

STRINE	ENGLISH
Egg nishner	Air-conditioner
Sex	Bags
Furry tiles	Stories told to children
Sander's lape	Resting deeply
Share	A spray of water

But Morrison wasn't finished. He later realized that some residents of England itself weren't in fact speaking English. A few at the very top of the social ladder were actually communicating via a language he named Fraffly, after this group's pronunciation of the English word *frightfully.* As with Strine, Afferbeck Lauder wrote a book, *Fraffly Well Spoken,* that guided outsiders in understanding this strange tongue. A few of his helpful translations:

FRAFFLY	ENGLISH
Fraffly caned a few	Frightfully kind of you
Nems	Names
Assay earl chep	I say, old chap
Egg wetter gree	I quite agree
Shomp yebble	Shan't be able
Orstrellion	A speaker of Strine

Fraffly well written, Professor Lauder!

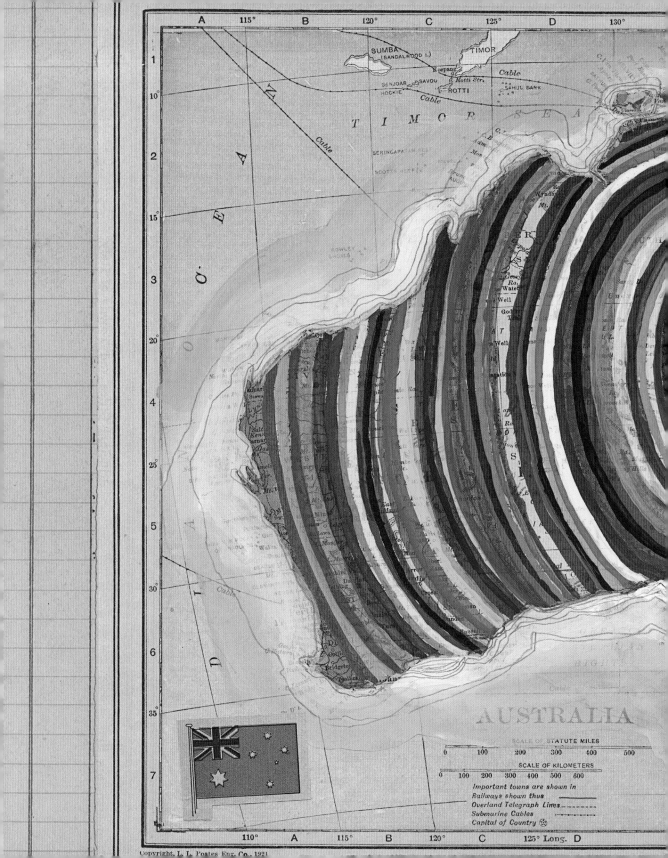

AUSTRALIA

SCALE OF STATUTE MILES

0   100   200   300   400   500

SCALE OF KILOMETERS

0   100   200   300   400   500   600

Important towns are shown thus
Railways shown thus
Overland Telegraph Lines
Submarine Cables
Capital of Country ⊛

WORLD ATLAS AND GAZETTEER

ARAFURA SEA

NEW GUINEA
BRITISH TER.)
Fly R.

TORRES STRAIT
MURRAY IS.

Mt. Yule
10,040
Mt. Owen Stanley
13,206
C. South East
PAPUA OR
NEW GUINEA
Hood Pt.

TROBRIAND IS.
WOODLARK I.
D'ENTRECASTEAUX
IS.
Orangerie B.

LOUISIADE
ARCHIPELAGO

CORAL SEA

OSPREY REEF

HOLMES REEF
WILLIS GROUP
CORINGA IS.
FLINDERS REEF
LIHOU REEF
AND CAYS
TREGROSSE IS.

PACIFIC OCEAN

STRINE

TASMANIA
FURNEAUX GROUP
Banks Str.

135° F 140° G 145° H 150° J
10°
15°
20°
25°
30°
35°
F 140° G 145° H 150° J 155° K

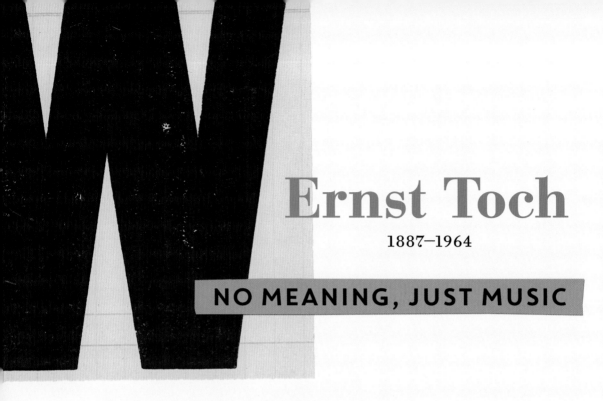

Ernst Toch

1887–1964

NO MEANING, JUST MUSIC

Say a word quickly twenty times in a row and it begins shedding its sense. What's left? Its sound.

Poets revel in the sound of words. Think of Robert Southey's "The Cataract of Lodore," a gushing celebration not only of a waterfall but of rhyme itself:

> *Advancing and prancing and glancing and dancing,*
> *Recoiling, turmoiling and toiling and boiling,*
> *And gleaming and streaming and steaming and beaming*

Or consider the poet Alastair Reid, who made lists of words whose sounds have the familiar flow of the numbers one through ten.

Ounce, dice, trice, quartz, quince, sago, serpent, oxygen,

nitrogen, denim

We've always loved the music of language. Why else remember "Peter Piper picked a peck of pickled peppers"? Certainly not for the meaning. Put on your backpacks, grab your ice axes, and let us follow those who've taken this road to distant destinations few have visited.

Take the 1916 poem "Karawane" by the German writer Hugo Ball, which begins:

> *jolifanto bambla ô falli bambla*
> *grossiga m'pfa habla horem*

The words? Made up. Meaning? Nonexistent. For Ball's generation, which had seen seemingly rational governments lead Europe into the bloodbath of World War I, making sense no longer made sense. In poetry and art, the Dada movement Ball helped found embraced the irrational.

Writing at the same time in Russia, Alexei Kruchenykh and Viktor Khlebnikov went so far as to invent an entire new sound language called Zaum. Though their words had no clear sense, they felt that sounds communicate meaning just as the colors and shapes of abstract art do. Allow me to try to recite "Dyr Bul Shchyl," the most famous Zaum poem:

Dyr bul shchyl

ubeshshchur

skum

vy so bu

r l ez.

Kruchenykh and Khlebnikov regarded it as a triumph. "In this five-line poem," they wrote, "there is more of the Russian national character than in all the poetry of Pushkin."

The invention of the tape recorder was a boon for sound poets. Suddenly they could alter the sounds of words in brand-new ways. Brion Gysin's "I Am That I Am" features every possible permutation of the words in that statement, his voice given eerie echoes, recorded over itself, and changing from glacially slow to so fast as to be barely perceptible.

But surely one of the oddest works built on the sounds of words is the work of our next subject. A toast to Ernst Toch!

Born in Vienna, he had an acute ear. Perhaps too acute. Excellent for the classical composer he grew into, but troublesome when it came to background noise, especially of a certain type. Streetcars, teakettles, ticking clocks? No problem. A pair of neighbors gossiping? Problem.

Why was this? Because speech is so similar to music. It has rhythm, pitch, crisscrossing melodies. Toch couldn't tune it out. Then came his cymbal clap of an idea. Why not make use of talk's musical side and turn his obstacle into his material? And so was born his *Gesprochene Musik,* "Spoken Music," performed by a chorus that speaks rather than sings.

But what do they speak? you ask. Everyday conversation?

You're on Toch's wavelength. He did indeed write a piece built from cocktail party chatter. But his most famous creation in this vein is his celebrated *Geographical Fugue.*

"What's a fugue?" asks the youngster. A composition in which all the musicians take turns with the melody, as when you're singing a round. Fugues sound like conversations in which everyone's talking at once. J. S. Bach was a whiz at writing them 250 years before Toch. Like the Oulipo writers, Toch took something old and made it new.

Why *geographical?* Because that's what he called for his chorus to speak: proper names from an atlas. He sifted those names for the sound and rhythm he wanted and wrote a piece that looks like a score for percussionists, showing rhythm but not pitch. It's arranged for a SATB chorus—sopranos, altos, tenors, and basses. It begins with the tenors declaiming:

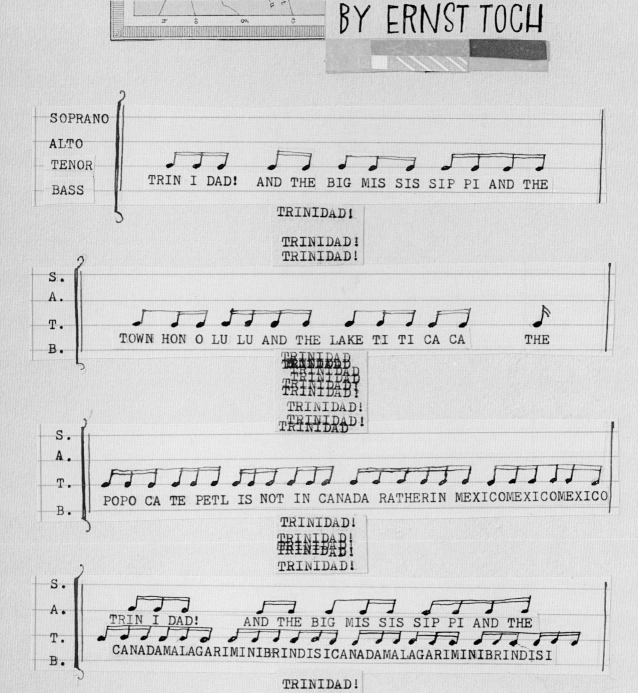

Trinidad!

And the big Mississippi

and the town Honolulu

and the lake Titicaca,

the Popocatepetl is not in Canada rather in Mexico Mexico Mexico

Then the altos do the same, followed by the sopranos, then the basses. Meanwhile, the other voices proclaim other geographical names, the lines woven like strands in a musical maypole. The piece builds to a rousing climax that ends where it began with *Trinidad!* A perfect fugue, following all the rules. Even Bach would be forced to give his approval.

The public certainly has. YouTube offers dozens of versions. Toch was a respected composer who moved to America and won a Pulitzer Prize for one of his seven symphonies. He regarded *Geographical Fugue* as a trifle and never could comprehend its success. Rhythm without melody? Words spoken but not sung? It sounds like an idea that'll never fly. Audience poison. A money loser.

True, young man. It sounds a lot like rap. Toch was onto something after all.

David Bryce

1845–1923

THE QUEST TO BE SMALLEST

You've heard of the golden mean—neither too much nor too little of anything. Why did the philosophers of old so often recommend this path? Because they knew that we're brain-on-fire extremists! Consult *Guinness World Records* for proof: fastest mile on a pogo stick, largest collection of airplane sickness bags, deepest underwater wedding.

No sooner had writing been invented than someone got the idea of trying to write smaller than anyone else. We know this from a four-thousand-year-old Sumerian cuneiform clay tablet measuring 1 5/16 by 1 5/8 inches. Homer's epic the *Iliad* is reported to have been copied in such small print that it fit inside the shell of a nut—quite possibly the origin of the phrase *in a nutshell.*

When Johannes Gutenberg pioneered printing with movable type in the 1450s, whole new possibilities opened up. Now that books didn't have to be written by hand, could they be smaller? Gutenberg Bibles were roughly seventeen inches high and twelve inches wide and weighed in at over fifty pounds. The race was on for a Bible as tiny as these were big.

Minibibliophiles define miniature books as those not exceeding three inches in height or width. Why make them? you might reasonably ask. To which I might reasonably ask in return whether anyone here owns an iPod. Small things make it possible to carry a lot in a pocket, be it a music collection or one's favorite prayers. Beyond that, there's the challenge. Miniature books demand the utmost of type founders, printers, papermakers, and binders.

So it was in 1486, just a few decades after Gutenberg burst onto the scene, that a Naples printer offered a prayer book measuring two by three inches. Why not a whole Bible? Lead type was too large and paper too thick for a work so long.

In 1674 the printer Benedikt Smidt moved to Amsterdam. By way of announcing his presence, he offered a poem about flowers as a leatherbound, gold-clasped book that measured a mere ½ by ⅜ inch — the size of a fingernail. This held the record for world's smallest book for the next two hundred years.

Typefaces shrank during that time. From twelve-point type,

commonly seen in books today, type founders got down to 4.5 points, then 2.5. In 1878, the Salmin brothers in Italy used two-point type, so small that its nickname remains *fly's eye.* With such a small font, they could print Dante's long *Divine Comedy* in miniature form, a work that took them eleven years to produce because the type was so frail it could be used only once. But not even they succeeded in printing a miniature Bible. The "thumb Bibles" that had been printed for two hundred years were all abridgements of the full work.

Enter our featured micromaniac, David Bryce!

A Glasgow publisher, he took advantage of photolithography, which let printers achieve smallness by printing from plates bearing photographic reductions of larger works. Nobody said miniature books had to be printed from type. Bryce also made use of new technology for making ultra-thin paper.

The result? His 1895 New Testament, ¾ by ⅝ inch. The following year, he was the first to produce a full miniature Bible, 876 pages long, 1¹³⁄₁₆ by 1¼ inches. It was bound in gilt-edged leather. In a pocket in the cover was a powerful magnifying glass. The goal had been reached!

One characteristic of extremists is that they don't like stopping. The Bible might have been miniaturized, but who could produce the smallest book, no matter the text?

TINY
ALPHABET
OF
ANIMALS
— GLASGOW —
David Bryce & Son

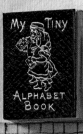

My Tiny
ALPHABET
BOOK

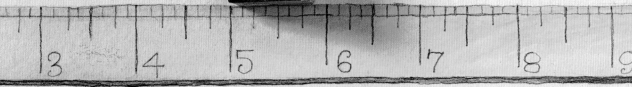

3   4   5   6   7   8   9

A
a for
ALBATROSS

T
t for
TIGER

O
o for
OWL

Z
z for
ZEBRA

The race continued. Fast-forward eighty years. We're now measuring not in inches but in millimeters. In 1978 Ian Macdonald of Scotland prints his *Three Blind Mice*—perhaps a comment on the eyestrain that goes with miniature printing. It measures 2.1 millimeters square, a new record.

But records are made to be broken. In 1996 a Russian printer produces Anton Chekhov's short story *A Chameleon* in an edition breaking the 1-millimeter barrier: .9 millimeters by .9 millimeters. *The Guinness Book of World Records* crowns him.

Then, in 2012, the Toppan Printing Company of Tokyo offers a book about Japanese flowers measuring .75 millimeters by .75 millimeters, produced with the same microprinting techniques used in making paper currency. A new record holder!

But wait. What's that whirring? Could it be the sound of Gutenberg revolving in his grave? He must have heard the news that nanotechnologists in Israel have put the entire Hebrew Bible on a single chip of silicon—it's half a millimeter square, no bigger than a poppy seed. No pages to turn. Instead of ink on paper, it was etched with a beam of ions. An astounding feat that comes with a problem: it needs to be magnified 10,000 times to be readable.

I believe I hear another sound: Gutenberg laughing.

Allen Read

1906–2002

IN SEARCH OF THE
TWO-LETTER HOLY GRAIL

People looking at a river might think of fishing, flooding, bird-watching, kayaking. But a few minds light up with the thought "I wonder where that river starts."

In the realm of geography, we call such people explorers. In language, they're called etymologists. Both live to track something back to its source. Their struggles are long and their travails many. In light of that, please offer your heartiest welcome to the curious, dogged, indefatigable Allen Walker Read!

His own beginning was in Winnebago, Minnesota, where he took an early interest in local place-names. Did *Winnebago* mean "people of the sea," as some claimed, suggesting that the Winnebago

Indians had made a long migration from one of the coasts? Words, he realized, weren't bland abstractions but carried the flesh and blood of history.

Not to mention other bodily products. One of Read's first studies was of writings he'd copied off bathroom walls and other public places on a tour of the West in 1928. For most, a witticism scratched into a picnic table is a defacement. For an etymologist, it's documentation, and more desirable rather than less if it carries a date. Read wrote up his findings but found that not everyone shared his gusto for language at its earthiest. With American publishers fearing laws against obscenity, the world's first scholarly collection of graffiti had to be printed in Paris.

A blizzard of books and papers followed — appropriate, as it was Read who'd traced the origin of the word *blizzard.* It was he again who'd found that the Rocky Mountains hadn't always worn that name but had earlier been known as the Enchanted Mountains, and the Shining Mountains before that, and the Stony Mountains before that. He tracked *Dixie* and *Podunk.* But it was another word of mysterious origins that captivated Read and obsessed his colleagues. To find its source once and for all was the Holy Grail of etymology. The word? *OK.*

A tiny two-letter tool of towering usefulness. The fourth word spoken on the moon, by astronaut Buzz Aldrin. A can-do word presumed to be American but now found worldwide, embodying American culture's innovation and spread. But it was a word without a birth certificate. Who thought it up? Where? When? Why?

The Englishmen who sought the source of the Nile battled malaria, native spears, and one another. Read's search was similarly long, strewn with dead ends and shadowed by rival explorers.

His first step was to judge other countries' claim to *OK*. American soldiers abroad during World War II were surprised to find the word already in use from the sidewalks of Japan to the sands of the Sahara. Was it indeed made in America?

Germans claimed it derived from the army rank known as *Oberst Kommandant.* The British thought it went back to Elizabethan English. The Greeks felt it came from *olla kalla,* meaning "all good." For the French, it derived from the Haitian port Aux Cayes, famed for the fine rum it exported, the word used as a mark of excellence in any sphere.

Read traveled these many roads and returned shaking his head. The claims lacked a sufficient store of what etymologists demand most: documentation. Verifiable uses of the word in newspapers, books, or other writings that would nail down when and where it was used, what it meant, and how it spread. Read rejected the foreign theories.

If the word indeed was American, the path wasn't clear but instead forked in a dozen directions. Did *OK* get its start as an abbreviation used by telegraph operators for *open key*? Was its source Orrin Kendall, a biscuit maker whose products, stamped with his initials, were beloved by Union soldiers during the Civil War? Did it originate with Old Keokuk, chief of the Sauk Indians, who signed treaties with *OK*? Did it come from the Choctaw word *okeh*? From President Andrew Jackson's mangled spelling of *all correct*?

Each of these theories had its backers. Read worked his way through their claims. He determined that the word had probably first appeared in the 1840s. But when, exactly? He combed newspapers of the period by the hundreds. Finally, he stumbled upon a source that was earlier than all the others, one that came with a new explanation. *OK* was short for *Old Kinderhook,* a phrase associated with President Martin Van Buren, from Kinderhook, New York, the word spreading outward from his reelection campaign of 1840. The oldest usage Read could find was March 23 of that year. The birth certificate had been found.

Triumphantly, he reported his findings. His colleagues considered his evidence and were won over. The riddle of *OK* had been solved.

And then came a bombshell—the discovery of a Boston businessman's handwritten diary that seemed to contain *OK*. Its year? 1815, a stunning twenty-five years earlier, exploding Read's theory. But there were problems. The letter *k* was indistinct. And if it was a *k,* the word *OK* made no sense in the sentence.

Look in a top-notch dictionary, and before a word's meaning you'll find the date and source of its first known use. While the search for *OK*'s first use was going on, Read and many others were working on a new dictionary of American English. One member of that team, Woodford Heflin by name, announced that the book would use the 1815 citation for *OK.*

Read was furious, feeling the diary's *OK* too suspect to be taken seriously. He journeyed to see the diary firsthand and examined the passage in question with a magnifying glass. His conclusion? The writer had paused in his sentence, causing a run of ink that resulted in a blob that transformed an *h* into a *k.* The dictionary's editor eventually agreed with him, but an academic battle ensued between Heflin and Read that flared for years.

Then, a new bombshell. Another scholar on the trail found a printed use that predated Read's by a month. It bore no connection to Old Kinderhook but rather meant "correct," as we use *OK* today. Then Read's rival Heflin found a still earlier use, from November of 1839. The case wasn't closed after all.

Read slogged further upstream through the rivers of newsprint. Browsing issues of the *Boston Morning Post* from 1838, he noticed something odd. There appeared to have been a fad for comic abbreviations that year. *G.C.* for *gin cocktail. G.T.D.H.D.* for *Give the Devil his due.* Not unlike today's *LOL* and other texting abbreviations.

The odd thing was that there was another newspaper craze at the same time, this one for intentional misspellings. *No use,* for instance, was rendered *Know yuse.* And then Read found it. The two fads converged on March 23, 1839. The result: *O.K.* for *oll korrect.*

Read had bested Heflin by seven months. More than forty years later, his record still stands.

Why should we take pleasure in abbreviations and misspellings? Human playfulness, Read would answer. It gives birth not only to sudoku and *Saturday Night Live,* but to words and phrases like *oll korrect.* Or the abbreviation I saw online only this morning: PCMCIA.

Its meaning? People Can't Memorize Computer Industry Acronyms.

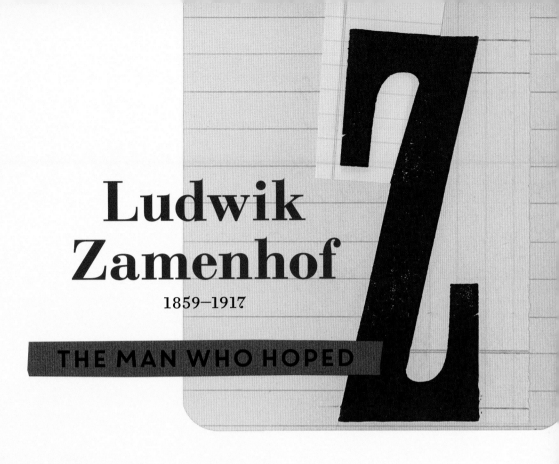

Ludwik Zamenhof

1859–1917

THE MAN WHO HOPED

Białystok is the setting for our last scene. A city in eastern Poland, part of the Russian Empire in the nineteenth century. A place where the war of all against all plays out daily in that era. The Poles hate the Russians, who hate the Germans, who hate the Lithuanians, who hate the Jews. Murders, mobs, burnings, beatings. In 1874 a teenage boy decides to try to end the war.

His name: Ludwik Zamenhof. His method: a common tongue, dissolving ignorance and ethnic feuds. An auxiliary language existing alongside the others, associated with no nation or people. The idea electrifies him.

He begins building a language that would make Descartes proud. His alphabet has twenty-eight letters. Every letter makes only one sound, and every sound is represented by only one letter. All words are accented on the next-to-last syllable. Nouns have no gender and all end in *o*. Adverbs end in *e*. Adjectives in *a*.

He profits from studying the easy grammar of English but avoids its many irregular verb endings. All his verbs are regular. To speak his language requires learning only sixteen rules.

He draws the roots of his new vocabulary from European languages. The overwhelming task of creating words for every object, concept, quality, and action is simplified by the use of endings: *Vido*, sight. *Vida*, visual. *Vide*, visually. *Vidi*, to see.

Prefixes and suffixes accomplish the same. The ending *-aro* indicates a collection. *Domo*, house. *Domaro*, a village. *Arbo*, tree. *Arbaro*, forest.

After more than a decade of refining, Zamenhof is ready. He describes his new language in a forty-page manuscript, but all books must be approved by the Russian censors, who are deeply suspicious of new ideas. Zamenhof's father happens to know one of the censors and convinces him that his son's booklet is harmless. It's published in 1887.

The work is titled *An International Language: Introduction and Complete Textbook for Russians*. Since Zamenhof decided against using his own name, the book's author is listed as Dr. Esperanto. In his language, the name means "one who hopes."

Letters from excited readers begin arriving. Zamenhof is amazed to see that some are actually written in his language. An oculist by day, he spends his nights translating his book, filling orders, corresponding. His language comes to be known as Esperanto.

Tolstoy, Russia's great novelist, reports reading in the language after only two hours of study. *La Esperantisto,* the first magazine in Esperanto, appears. An Esperanto hymn is composed. Textbooks and dictionaries are published. Clubs and societies spring up in Spain, Japan, Peru, the United States.

To disprove the charge that an artificial tongue can't be literary, Zamenhof writes poems in Esperanto. He translates Dickens, Tolstoy, Shakespeare. What does the language look and sound like? An actor speaking Hamlet's famous soliloquy would begin, *"Ĉu esti aŭ ne esti—tiel staras nun la demando."*

In 1905 the first Universal Congress of Esperantists meets in France. Inside the auditorium flies the Esperanto flag, its five-pointed star representing the five major continents.

"Through the air of our hall mysterious sounds are traveling," Zamenhof tells the crowd. "The sound of something great that is now being born."

To make changes in a natural language that's evolved over centuries is almost impossible because no one is in charge. Zamenhof finds himself with the opposite problem. Changing a created language is too easy.

One Esperantist writes a letter to Zamenhof demanding the accent marks be removed. There are complaints about points of grammar, pronunciation, the source of word roots.

A prominent French supporter loses his bid for reform and withdraws from the movement, promoting his revision of Esperanto, called Ido. Many Esperantists follow him. They publish their own magazine, *La Progreso.*

To Zamenhof this isn't progress, but disaster. Accusations and insults fly between the two camps. Meanwhile bombs and bullets fly between Russia and Japan. The Americans and the Spanish. The Turks and the Greeks. The Italians and the Abyssinians. The Boers and the British. A universal tongue is needed more than ever.

August 1914. World War I breaks out. Everything Zamenhof has struggled against — rabid nationalism, the lure of aggression, the demonization of others — is vigorously promoted by every government involved. His younger brother, ordered to fight in the Russian army, kills himself rather than take another's life. Zamenhof, already in poor health, grows weaker.

The Russian army has barely enough bullets and bread. Mass

mutinies of those opposed to the fighting take place. The army responds by executing pacifists. Zamenhof steadily declines.

In April of 1917, after two and a half years of war, the founder of Esperanto takes his last breath.

Am I going to end this parade on such a somber note?

Not entirely. Because Esperanto didn't die with Zamenhof. Today there are several million speakers of the language. They have websites, chat rooms, magazines, meetups. You can read Wikipedia in Esperanto and put your thoughts into it through Google Translate.

More important, in the century after Zamenhof, an even more widely used international language has come to the fore.

"Ido?" asks the gentleman. No, not Ido. English!

The official language of one-third of the world's countries. The unofficial language of pop music and film, TV and computing, science and business. Most of the Internet is in English. It's the common language that pilots and control towers use for international flights.

Understandable, given its wide dispersal via the British Empire and American movies. And though its spelling and pronunciation are a challenge, its grammar is among the world's easiest. Its nouns don't have gender. Its alphabet is simple compared with many scripts. Unlike tonal languages, it doesn't use pitch to distinguish meanings.

Still, English is anything but neutral, being associated strongly with Great Britain and the United States. And rather than an auxiliary tongue, as Zamenhof envisioned Esperanto, English has swallowed up countless languages, including many that Jessie Little Doe Baird and her fellow rescuers are struggling to save. Best not to imagine Zamenhof springing back to life and beholding its triumph.

On the other hand, Frederic Cassidy would be delighted to find the *Dictionary of American Regional English* completed at last. Jean-Dominique Bauby would discover *The Diving Bell and the Butterfly* in bookstores and libraries worldwide. Ignatius Donnelly's beliefs about Shakespeare may be out of favor, but his farsighted predictions of radio and TV in his novels have come true. Simon Vostre would thrill to see his gorgeously produced books guarded in climate-controlled rooms.

Think of words as grain. Most people grind it to make bread. But a few figured out how to turn it into whiskey. Such are the luminaries I've brought before you today. May each of you leave with your spirit warmed, your curiosity kindled, and your sense of the possible expanded. And now, farewell. I've got an Esperanto class to go to. Adiaŭ!

HELLO
SALUTON
GOODBYE
ADIOS SLÁN TOTSIENS ZDRAV!
SBOHEM ADJÖ
NAMASTE SAYONARA
KHUDA HAFIZ
DONADAGOHVI
ADIAU!
GOODBYE

SOURCE NOTES

DANIEL NUSSBAUM

p. 2: "INTHE BEGINNG . . . FERSUR": Nussbaum, p. 11.

p. 2: "ONCEPON . . . 1LITL1": Ibid., p. 24.

p. 2: "BHOLD MMOI!": Ibid., p. 19.

p. 2: "2BORWAT?": Ibid., p. 49.

p. 2: "MYMYMY IMSOGQ": Ibid., p. 84.

p. 2: "THEGR81 . . . 2DMAAX": Ibid., p. 72.

p. 4: "GESSWAT! . . . ISWEAR!": Ibid., pp. 66–67.

p. 4: "HEYDIG! . . . SEEEE": Ibid., p. 53.

JEAN-DOMINIQUE BAUBY

p. 7: "Meticulous people . . . can exist": Bauby, p. 22.

p. 7: "In one section . . . guilty conscience": Ibid., p. 31.

pp. 7–8: "Sunday . . . than usual": Ibid., p. 100.

p. 8: "Our farewells . . . of my past": Ibid., p. 120.

p. 8: "A very black fly . . . compared to this": Ibid., p. 102.

pp. 8–9: "On good days . . . far-off country": Ibid., pp. 40–41.

p. 9: "Depending on my mood . . . of my head": Ibid., pp. 36–37.

p. 9: "My mind . . . still-sleeping face": Ibid., p. 5.

p. 11: "I am fond . . . dance for me": Ibid., p. 19.

THOMAS URQUHART

p. 13: "I could have inserted . . . and subjection": Urquhart, p. 292.

p. 14: "vaulting, swimming . . . angling, shooting": Ibid., p. 397.

p. 14: "Thus for a while . . . inspection of either": Ibid., p. 236.

p. 16: "The greatest wonder . . . easiest to learn": Ibid., p. 205.

JESSIE LITTLE DOE BAIRD

p. 20: "Reclaiming our language . . . the creator": Quoted at Wôpanâak Language Reclamation Project website homepage, http://www.wlrp.org/.

IGNATIUS DONNELLY

p. 32: "Francis Bacon, Nicholas Bacon's son": Donnelly, p. 287.

p. 32: "Shak'st spur . . . word of them": Quoted in Fellows, p. 177.

p. 34: "Will I am . . . this play": Nicholson, pp. 37–38.

p. 34: "Don nill . . . this play": Walsh, p. 161.

ROSS ECKLER

p. 39: "This sentence contains . . . only one *z*": Quoted in Eckler, p. 225.

FREDERIC CASSIDY

p. 43: "What do you call . . . when it rains?": *Dictionary of American Regional English,* vol. 1, pp. 52, 61, and 65.

ROBERT SHIELDS

pp. 52–56: Robert Shields diary entries: Quoted in Isay, pp. 28–30.

p. 55: "It's gotten . . . never happened": Quoted in Kit Boss, "A Life, Single Spaced," *Seattle Times,* May 15, 1994.

MIKE GOLD

p. 65: "Every letter is endowed . . . little poem": Erik Lindegren, *An ABC-book* (New York: Pentalic, 1976), p. 54.

CORÍN TELLADO

p. 77: "Some months . . . imply things": Quoted in "Corín Tellado," *The Guardian*, May 3, 2009.

RAYMOND QUENEAU

p. 80: "Bastille Day" by Harry Matthews: Queneau et al., p. 20.

p. 82: "It isn't happiness . . . experience": Raymond Queneau, *The Bark-Tree*, trans. Barbara Wright (London: Calder and Boyars, 1968), p. 95. Originally published as *Le chiendent* (Paris: Librairie Gallimard, 1933).

GEORGES PEREC

p. 86: "Incurably insomniac . . . paragraph or two": Perec, p. 3.

SIMON VOSTRE

p. 90: "Whoever steals . . . the Rhine": Quoted in Drogin, p. 89.

p. 90: "If you do not know . . . all over": Ibid., p. 21.

p. 90: "Therefore, O reader . . . and the book": Ibid., p. 18.

p. 92: "If anyone take . . . Amen" and "For him that stealeth . . . him forever": Ibid., p. 88.

p. 93: "I have arranged . . . in the land": Ibid., pp. 52–53.

HOWARD CHACE

p. 95: "Wants pawn term . . . cordage": Chace, p. 19.

p. 95: "Yonder nor . . . strainers": Ibid., p. 22.

p. 97: "Bean ware the jumbo wok, Mason": Jan Anderson quoted in Ross A. Eckler, "Anguish Languish," *Word Ways* 30, no. 4 (1997): p. 276.

p. 97: "Jacques Aingell . . . Affe Tarr": Jay Ames, "Nymo Rhymes," *Word Ways* 10, no. 1 (1977): p. 16.

ROBERT McCORMICK

p. 102: "We insist . . . trodden before!": Thomas Lounsbury, "The Problem of Spelling Reform," *Century Illustrated Monthly* 25, no. 3 (November 1882): p. 283.

MARY ELLEN SOLT

p. 105: "Writing free verse . . . net down": Robert Frost, "An Address at Milton Academy," May 17, 1935.

p. 107: "Zinnia": Solt, p. 6.

ERNST TOCH

p. 115: "Ounce . . . denim": Reid, p. 39.

p. 115: "jolifanto . . . horem": Hugo Ball, *Ball and Hammer: Hugo Ball's Tenderenda the Fantast*, trans. Jonathan Hammer (New Haven: Yale University Press, 2002), p. 82.

p. 116: "Dyr bul shchyl . . . r l ez": Quoted in Gerald Janecek, *Zaum: The Transrational Poetry of Russian Futurism* (San Diego: San Diego University Press, 1996), p. 69.

p. 116: "In this five-line . . . Pushkin": Ibid., p. 57.

LUDWIK ZAMENHOF

p. 135: "Ĉu esti aŭ . . . la demando": Quoted in Okrent, p. 104.

p. 135: "Through the air . . . being born": Quoted in Joan Acocella, "A Language to Unite Humankind," *The New Yorker*, October 31, 2016, http://www.newyorker.com/magazine/2016/10/31/a-language-to-unite-humankind.

FURTHER ENTERTAINMENT

DANIEL NUSSBAUM

Nussbaum, Daniel. *PL8SPK: California Vanity Plates Retell the Classics.* New York: HarperCollins, 1993.

JEAN-DOMINIQUE BAUBY

Bauby, Jean-Dominique. *The Diving Bell and the Butterfly.* Translated by Jeremy Leggatt. New York: Knopf, 1997.

The Diving Bell and the Butterfly (film). Directed by Julian Schnabel. Paris: Pathé Renn Productions, 2007. DVD. A powerful rendering of Bauby's story, seen literally through his eye.

THOMAS URQUHART

Urquhart, Thomas. *The Works of Sir Thomas Urquhart.* Reprint, Glasgow, Scotland: Maitland Club, 1834. https://archive.org/details /worksofsirthomas00mait.

JESSIE LITTLE DOE BAIRD

Abley, Mark. *Spoken Here: Travels Among Threatened Languages.* Boston: Houghton Mifflin, 2003.

Harrison, K. David. *The Last Speakers: The Quest to Save the World's Most Endangered Languages.* Washington, D.C.: National Geographic, 2010.

The Linguists (film). Directed by Seth Kramer, Daniel A. Miller, and Jeremy Newberger. Garrison, NY: Ironbound Films, 2008. DVD. A chance to ride, hike, and listen with David Harrison and Greg Anderson as they seek out endangered language hotspots before time runs out.

We Still Live Here: Âs Nutayuneân (film). Directed by Anne Makepeace. Oley, PA: Bullfrog Films, 2010. A documentary about Jessie Baird's work to save the Wampanoag language.

Wôpanâak Language Reclamation Project. http://www.wlrp.org/.

MARC OKRAND

Klingon Language Institute. http://www.kli.org/.

Okrand, Marc. *The Klingon Dictionary.* New York: Pocket, 1985.

Okrent, Arika. *In the Land of Invented Languages.* New York: Spiegel and Grau, 2010. A fascinating journey led by a writer with a first-level certification in Klingon.

Schoen, Lawrence, and Andrew Stradev, trans. *The Klingon Hamlet (Star Trek).* New York: Pocket, 2001.

IGNATIUS DONNELLY

Donnelly, Ignatius. *The Cipher in the Plays and on the Tombstone.* St. Albans, U.K.: Verulam, 1899.

Fellows, Virginia M. *The Shakespeare Code.* Gardiner, MT: Snow Mountain Press, 2006.

Nicholson, Alexander. *No Cipher in Shakespeare.* London: T. Fisher Unwin, 1888.

Shapiro, James. *Contested Will: Who Wrote Shakespeare?* New York: Simon & Schuster, 2010. A look at the varied candidates and impulses behind the authorship controversy.

Walsh, William S. *Handy-Book of Literary Curiosities.* Philadelphia: Lippincott, 1893.

ROSS ECKLER

Eckler, Ross. *Making the Alphabet Dance.* New York: St. Martin's, 1997.

Word Ways: The Journal of Recreational Linguistics. www.wordways.com/.

FREDERIC CASSIDY

Dictionary of American Regional English, 5 vols. Cambridge, MA: Belknap Press, 1985–2012. Available in larger public libraries and most college libraries. http://www.daredictionary.com/.

DORIS CROSS

Altered books. http://altered-book.com/arts-and-crafts.html has much information on book-altering techniques. An image search for "Altered books" will show you the range of what's being done.

Cross, Doris. *Col-umns.* San Francisco: Trike, 1982. Extremely rare. You can see some of her work online at http://www.poetryfoundation.org/harriet/2014/04/who-is-doris-cross/ and http://www.thing.net/~grist/l&d/dcross02.htm.

Dillard, Annie. *Mornings Like This: Found Poems.* New York: Harper Perennial, 1996.

The Found Poetry Review. http://www.foundpoetryreview.com/.

Holmes, Janet. *The ms of m y kin.* Exeter, U.K.: Shearsman, 2009.

Phillips, Tom. *A Humument: A Treated Victorian Novel.* 5th ed. London: Thames & Hudson, 2012. See also http://www.tomphillips.co.uk/.

ROBERT SHIELDS

Isay, David, and Harvey Wang. *Holding On: Dreamers, Visionaries, Eccentrics, and Other American Heroes.* New York: Norton, 1997.

SVEN JACOBSON

Jacobson, Sven. *Unorthodox Spelling in American Trademarks.* Stockholm: Almqvist & Wiksell, 1966.

MIKE GOLD

Cicale, Annie. *The Art and Craft of Hand Lettering.* New York: Lark Books, 2004. For inspiration and instruction in calligraphy, this is a great place to start.

Sacks, David. *Letter Perfect: The Marvelous History of Our Alphabet from A to Z.* New York: Broadway, 2003.

DAVID WALLACE

Dunham, Will. "Toil and Trouble: Researchers Link Shakespeare to Disputed Play." Reuters, April 10, 2015. http://www.reuters.com/article/2015/04/11/us-science-shakespeare-idUSKBN0N128W20150411.

Juola, Patrick. "How a Computer Program Helped Reveal J. K. Rowling Wrote *A Cuckoo's Calling.*" *Scientific American,* August 20, 2013. https://www.scientificamerican.com/article/how-a-computer-program-helped-show-jk-rowling-write-a-cuckoos-calling/.

BOHUMIL HRABAL

Hrabal, Bohumil. *Dancing Lessons for the Advanced in Age.* New York: Harcourt, 1995.

CORÍN TELLADO

The author's massive output has not yet been translated into English. Her Wikipedia page may list more titles than any other author entry on the site: https://en.wikipedia.org/wiki/Corín_Tellado.

RAYMOND QUENEAU

Queneau, Raymond, et al. *Oulipo Laboratory,* trans. Harry Matthews and Iain White. London: Atlas, 1995. A sampling of Oulipo works.

GEORGES PEREC

Bellos, David. *Georges Perec: A Life in Words.* New York: Random House, 1993.

Perec, Georges. *A Void,* trans. Gilbert Adair. Boston: Godine, 2005.

SIMON VOSTRE

Drogin, Marc. *Anathema! Medieval Scribes and the History of Book Curses.* Totowa, NJ: Schram, 1983.

HOWARD CHACE

Chace, Howard. *Anguish Languish.* Englewood Cliffs, NJ: Prentice Hall, 1956.

Hulme, John. *Mörder Guss Reims: The Gustav Leberwurst Manuscript.* New York: Potter, 1981.

Van Rooten, Luis d'Antin. *Mots d'heures: Gousses, Rames: The D'Antin Manuscript.* New York: Penguin, 1980.

ROBERT McCORMICK

Wolman, David. *Righting the Mother Tongue: From Olde English to Email, the Tangled Story of English Spelling.* New York: HarperCollins, 2008.

MARY ELLEN SOLT

Apollinaire, Guillaume. *Calligrammes: Poems of Peace and War (1913–1916),* trans. Anne Hyde Greet. Berkeley: University of California Press, 2004.

Higgins, Dick. *Pattern Poetry: Guide to an Unknown Literature.* Albany: State University of New York Press, 1987.

Solt, Mary Ellen. *Flowers in Concrete.* Bloomington: Indiana University Press, 1966. The book is rare, but its images can be viewed at http://www.ubu .com/historical/solt/solt_flowers.html.

A. A. MORRISON

Lauder, Afferbeck. *Fraffly Well Spoken: How to Speak the Language of London's West End.* Sydney: Ure Smith, 1968.

———. *Let Stalk Strine: A Lexicon of Modern Strine Usage.* Sydney: Ure Smith, 1965.

ERNST TOCH

Gysin, Brion. *Back in No Time: The Brion Gysin Reader,* ed. Jason Weiss. Middletown, CT: Wesleyan University Press, 2002. You can hear Gysin reading "I Am That I Am" at http://www.ubu.com/sound /gysin.html.

Reid, Alastair. *Ounce Dice Trice.* New York: New York Review Children's Collection, 2009.

Toch, Ernst. *Geographical Fugue for Speaking Chorus.* The score is available from Alfred Music, http://www.alfred.com/geographical -fugue/p/00-60168/.

DAVID BRYCE

Bromer, Anne, and Julian I. Edison. *Miniature Books: 4,000 Years of Tiny Treasures.* New York: Abrams, 2007. Filled with gorgeous color photos.

Miniature Book Society. http://mbs.org/index.html.

ALLEN READ

Read, Allen Walker. *Classic American Graffiti.* Santa Rosa, CA: Maledicta, 1977.

Stacey, Michelle. "At Play in the Language." *The New Yorker,* September 4, 1989, pp. 51–74. A profile of Read.

LUDWIK ZAMENHOF

Bryson, Bill. *The Mother Tongue: English and How It Got That Way.* New York: Morrow, 1990. An entertaining history of English that includes its emergence as a world language.

Esperanto-USA. This group offers instruction, groups, travel opportunities, and much else. https://www.esperanto-usa.org/. To start learning the language right away, see http://en.lernu.net/.

Okrent, Arika. *In the Land of Invented Languages.* New York: Spiegel and Grau, 2010.

UVW X